Breakth

C000260946

A Blueprint for your Mind

BRIAN COSTELLO

RIVERCLYDE

BOOKS

Published by Riverclyde Books

An imprint of Saltire Books Ltd

20 Main Street, Busby, Glasgow G76 8DU, Scotland

books@saltirebooks.com

First published 2016

Typeset in the UK by Type Study, Scarborough in 10/13pt Novarese
Printed and bound in the UK by TJ International Ltd, Padstow

ISBN 978–1–908127–24–2

A catalogue record for this book is available from the British library.

Project management: Lee Kayne
Editorial: Steven Kayne and Katy McColl
Illustrations: Matt Canning
Cover design: Phil Barker

Contents

CHAPTER 5   The conscious witness   149

We spend so much time in our own 'bubble' that we often can't appreciate how the world looks to others. The power for massive change lies in developing 'bubble jumping' skills and using them at just the right time.

CHAPTER 6   Just being you   183

One of the most difficult things we are ever asked to do is to just be ourselves. So, who are you . . . and how do you know if you are the 'right' you? Or the best you? Or you at all? Learn the skills of developing your own personal identity and proudly stamping it on the world.

To S.

Love G.

Foreword

It is a pleasure for me to write the foreword for Brian's book. I first met Brian a couple of years ago when he and Steven Burns brought me to Glasgow to train some of their students for a day on using language to help people make permanent changes in their life. I'm lucky enough to travel and teach all over the world on NLP, Coaching and Influence so I've met many different trainers out there.

Brian's infectious enthusiasm and passion was immediately contagious. In the world of personal development, there are people who 'get it' and people who don't. I could see straight away that Brian 'got it'. I very much believe that what you will read here has got a tremendous amount of potential to help you change your life.

This book is an extremely important book. It addresses the concept of a breakthrough and how to transform your life by breaking through the problems and challenges that are in your way. Often, such a breakthrough happens as a result of something simple. Someone says something and instantly, we think about things differently. We get an experience of something and we can never again see it in the same way. These breakthroughs are magical and help us to manifest the kind of lives we want.

But in our lives, such events are few and far between. We can never know the moment that our lives are changed, that our destiny is created. We move through this world at a relentless pace and we attempt to navigate the landscape of problems and difficulties as best we can, always moving forward toward our ultimate destinations. But the problem is that we can become stuck in the past, trapped by our own fears and limiting beliefs. We can get lost in the uncertainty of the coming future. The very thing we want can be guarded by the antagonistic forces of our own mind.

Brian's book is a great opportunity for you to battle these forces in such a way that you can take charge of your life and build your future. The ability to break through problems lies in your ability to learn to think differently. The map to follow is explained in these pages as Brian gives you an understanding of how your mind works and explains what you need to do in order to make your mind work for you.

When people talk about change, they often describe it as a long drawn out process. The idea is that it is a culmination of continuous and deliberate effort applied over time which may eventually lead to long-term change. Although this may sometimes be the case, the reality is that often powerful change happens in an instant. It happens not just because we become aware of what we are doing. It happens because we get the chance to shift perspective.

In many ways that's what a breakthrough is . . . it is a changing of perspective. But it is instant . . . immediate . . . unforgettable. It is the ultimate moment of insight which means you can no longer look at the situation in the same way. This book may well be called Breakthroughs rather than Breakthrough because Brian guides you through multiple perspective shifts. He helps you understand the variety of ways that you can think about events and how to start choosing better ways of thinking about them.

The fundamentals of trigger, thought, feeling and action are extremely simple in nature. At the same time, they are crucial in terms of their importance in transformation. Understanding that the world only impacts us through how we interpret it means that we can get the opportunity to build a better way of interpreting it.

The benefits of this aren't just confined to a healthier sense of well being and contentment. They aren't just confined to a happier sense of self and an increased feeling of motivation. They aren't just confined to a wonderful sense of relaxation and feeling that we can handle whatever life throws at us. Instead, the benefits of taking charge over how we interpret the world extends to our outer world. They help us make better decisions which in turn lead to better action which in turn leads to a better life.

Making breakthroughs in the various areas of your life will help you to create a better future from the ground up. So often, we spend time focusing on how tough things are or how unfair things are or how impossible things are. When you get to see things anew, you are given the gift of realising that you have more control than you could ever possibly know. The real trick is to find a new way of thinking about the problems in your life.

NLP or Neuro-Linguistic Programming is one of the foundational tools used throughout this book. It offers you the chance to reprogram the way you see the world. Through Brian's simple explanations, you will discover easy ways to apply this ground-breaking tool to your life. Whether it is in learning how to create the best kinds of emotional states to be in more of the time or a case of changing a habit or non-useful behaviour, this book will provide you with what you need to change your psychological patterns and achieve what you want. Remember that the exercises are critical. It is vital that you apply the learning for it to make a difference.

Breakthrough isn't really a noun. It is a verb and a preposition. It is so, so important that you treat it as such. If you do, you can use this book to say goodbye to the problems which stopped you from being all you could be, and you too can live the ultimate, wonderful life that you were born to live.

Owen Fitzpatrick
Co-Author of The Ultimate Introduction to NLP
www.owenfitzpatrick.com

Preface

Let me take you back in time to 2007, just a few short years after I had first encountered the world of Personal Development. In those years, I read countless books on therapy, hypnosis and psychology and absolutely nothing else. I had become a 'walking encyclopedia' bursting with techniques, knowledge and information but with absolutely no idea of what the hell to do with it all!

Then, in 2007, I mistakenly ordered what I would class as my first 'self help' book. It was by an author called Michael Neill and was entitled *Feel Happy Now*.[1] I say 'mistakenly ordered' as I was expecting another textbook! To my surprise, it was far from it and, although I wouldn't say it changed my life, it was a revelation that definitely changed my reading.

A million miles away from the dry text books and seminar transcripts I had been used to, Michael's informal style of writing drew me in and refused to let go. I was amazed by the ease with which he took challenging concepts and explained them clearly, distilling everything down to a simple message. I was hooked on his style and, to this day, Michael's early books remain a huge influence on my writing, presenting and work with clients.

---

[1] Neill M. *Feel Happy Now: Small changes that make a huge difference*. London: Hay House UK. 2007.

The core message of *Feel Happy Now* really was a revelation to me. Stop waiting to change before you allow yourself to feel happy . . . *feel* happy now and change *because* you are happy. No one had ever told me it was possible to be happy even if my life wasn't in perfect harmony. I enthusiastically embraced this idea and continue to share it with my clients, course delegates, friends and family.

Fast forward to 2008 and an even bigger change was in store for me. I experienced my first live Tony Robbins event and I watched in awe as the master of his field made the world of change seem effortless with his simple, clear and powerful messages.

Sometime during the weekend I noticed that I had been scribbling notes on the inside cover of my notebook. I was so inspired that, almost without realising, I had begun to sketch out ideas for a course that would deliver my take on what Tony was doing. I knew then that it would be life changing.

Those notes were eventually moulded into the very first Breakthrough Weekend that I ever delivered and, in the years since, this course has helped countless people make massive changes in their lives – we have changed careers, transformed relationships, seen people move to the other side of the planet, made new friendships and too many other changes to list. My intention has always been to help people live happier and more fulfilled lives and, this course gives everyone who comes along the chance of his or her very own Breakthrough.

Over the last year I have taken all the concepts I teach on the Breakthrough Weekend, the simple understandings, powerful messages and useful techniques that help to change lives, and distilled them into the book that you are holding in your hands. This is the Breakthrough book.

If I achieve anything in this book I hope to build on the work of Michael and Tony and make the concept of the mind, emotions and why we do the things we do, accessible and easy to understand. I hope you understand that you too can achieve a Breakthrough – that beautiful moment of clarity when you realise that it's actually possible for you to take a hold of your life and change it. There is a Breakthrough in this book for you . . . but the book alone can't make that happen. The book cannot change your life without you getting up and doing something with the things you learn. Because there is no change without some action. It doesn't have to be a huge action – the smallest step forward is still a step in the right direction, but it is important to understand that you are the only one that can take that step.

To help you integrate the concepts in the book, I have designed some exercises. Now, I realise that there are very few people hungry enough for change to grab a pen and paper and sit down for an hour to write out a list of their top 100 goals, so I have designed (almost) every exercise to have different levels. If you are really up for change, you can take your time and write everything out but it can be just as valuable for you to do the exercises silently and effortlessly in your head, which is useful if you are sitting on the bus or are just one of those people who simply can't be bothered writing anything down! I'll let you into a wee secret – I'm one of those people!

I'll leave it up to you to decide how much you want to commit to the exercises throughout the book, but I promise you that, if you allow yourself the space to spend a few minutes thinking about them, writing them or whatever you choose to do with them, you will discover the value. As I always say when I welcome delegates to the course that inspired this book, it is in the *doing* rather than just the *thinking*, that we create the Breakthrough.

Though their names and other small details have been changed to protect identities, I thank the 6 people whose stories 'top and tail' each chapter. I know that their stories and their commitment to change will inspire you as much as they did me.

I really do hope you enjoy the book, I hope I live up to the standards set by my heroes and mentors and I hope that you find your Breakthrough.

Do good things.

Brian Costello
Glasgow, Scotland
December 2015

Acknowledgements

I would like to thank all the people who have supported, encouraged and been excited about the writing of this book. Even if you have not been singled out for a personal mention, I promise that each and every one of you, has been a source of energy that has helped when things didn't make sense, when I lost my way or when my brain went fuzzy.

Special thanks goes to my family, Sheena, Jodie and Amy, who lost me for many Sundays and many more evenings as I sat with my head in the laptop trying to find the right way to say the things I already knew. Thank you for the hidden post-it notes of encouragement. They mean the world.

And a wee nod upstairs to my Dad. A man who always had a belief that even though you may have been poor, you could always be happy. The first coach I ever had. I'm on my adventure.

Thanks to all my coaches, teachers and mentors over the last 12 years of learning. Particularly Michael Neill, Richard Bandler, my trainers John Grinder & Tony Robbins and many others whose influences, stories, skills and knowledge are distilled on these pages. I hope this does you proud.

To Owen Fitzpatrick, my gratitude for taking time out of your crazy schedule to write the Foreword to this book. Your support, belief and encouragement means a hell of a lot in this crazy world we work in! HH.

A huge bundle of thanks must be sent to Lee Kayne. Honestly mate, without you this would still just be an idea. I may not have liked your deadlines but as a source of never-ending enthusiasm, encouragement, kind words and the occasional kick up the backside, your support through this has been awesome. Thank you.

Additional thanks to Steven Kayne & Katy McColl for reading endless edits of the book and giving your input, expertise and direction. You may have been behind the scenes but I knew you were there and it's great to have such a team behind me.

Although we have never met, a big thank you to Phil for designing the cover. Four quick possibilities, favourite picked and just two rounds of tweaks later, we had a cover that everyone is going nuts over! Amazing stuff. Likewise, thanks to Dave for the beautiful page design and Matt for the illustrations. Cheers to all of you for your time, talent and efforts.

And finally, thanks to all my clients, delegates on my courses and everyone else who has allowed me the privilege to walk into their lives and make a change. You have all taught me so much and without your trust in me, I could never have become the coach I am today.

This book is about you.

The big, fat, greasy slob

During our initial phone call, Jodie described herself as having been 'seriously depressed' for some time. She told me that, despite being madly in love with her wonderful husband, having an enjoyable and fulfilling job and a fantastic group of friends who care for her as much as she cares for them, she felt trapped in darkness and despair.

Jodie said that she didn't deserve any of the amazing things in her life and even having good people around her made her feel bad. She believed she was holding them back and hurting them simply by her presence in their lives. For example, why would someone as perfect as her husband want to marry her? Similar beliefs overshadowed her other relationships with family and friends.

She believed herself to be, in her own words, a 'big, fat, greasy slob', wasting her life, her husband's life and the lives of everyone who knew her.

We arranged to meet a few days later. My guess after the initial call was that I would be helping Jodie address some weight issues and get over a period of depression.

I arrived at the office on the day of our appointment to find a tall, slim mystery lady with long, dark hair and big brown eyes waiting for me. Her clothes, make up and general appearance were impeccable. I didn't know who she was but she couldn't possibly be the client who had described herself as a 'big, fat, greasy slob'!

'Hi, you must be Brian' she said and flashed a big, friendly smile. 'I'm Jodie, nice to meet you.' This very attractive lady was indeed my 'slob'!

1

Searching for change

WHY DON'T WE JUST CHANGE?

Almost everyone wants to change something in their lives. It may be something big or something small but there is always something. As people we seem to be 'programmed' never to be 100% content and happy. We are always looking for something to be better. It's what makes us special.

If we weren't programmed this way then we would still be sitting round little fires in big caves in Africa! One day, some ancient person stood up and said "I'm pretty bored with painting on these walls, I'm going to go over there and see if there is something new". Those first brave steps into the unknown are the first steps in all of our histories.

But today, right here, right now, we have reached a stage where it isn't quite so easy to venture into the unknown. We have become accustomed to sticking with 'comfortable'.

This is why, when we modern, evolved folk want to change something, we find it tough to pull on our big boy or girl pants, pull up our socks and just . . . you know . . . *change*.

Wouldn't life be easier if we just realised that we are doing something stupid, annoying, destructive, ridiculous or all of the above and that we should stop, have a damn good word with ourselves and change our lives entirely?

So why don't we?

Is it because we can't? Is it because we don't want to? Is it because we want, in some bizarre way, to live life this way, feeling this crap? Is it because we deserve it? Is it because this is the way we are born and it can't actually be any other way?

Or is it because we have lost the ability to make our mind do anything other than what it is already doing? Are we simply stuck in a loop that we don't know how to stop?

Could it be that the reason so many people are stuck in situations they don't want to be in, feeling feelings they don't want to feel, doing things they don't want to do is because they have never been shown how to do anything else? Could it really be that simple?

I mean, why do we spend so long studying physics, maths and geography at school and no time at all studying ourselves? Why isn't there a teacher that can show us how to navigate the minefield of our emotions and our psyche? Why don't we come with instructions?

A manual entitled 'How to operate your Susan' or 'A beginners guide to working your Gordon', would be really damn useful, don't you agree?

Sadly though this is not the reality. I have two kids and I promise you, I checked everywhere the day they were born and it quickly became apparent that mini people (commonly known as 'babies' and subsequently 'children') do not come with instructions. And that leads us to one simple truth – that we are at the mercy of the world and we need to make sense of it ourselves.

LET THE WORLD WORK IT OUT

Let me show you what I think would be in the instruction book if one existed. Which it should. But it doesn't.

HUMAN MIND v2.3 – Instructions

The human mind now in your possession, is a delicate machine, completely at the mercy of the outside world. It is constantly vulnerable to the outside world. That outside world is a bitch of a thing which, without reason or warning, can turn round and smack you square in the face with an experience which, again for no reason at all, will cause your body to be filled with horrible feelings. These feelings are commonly called 'emotions'. You have no control over this at all. It would be good to be able to prepare for this. You can't. It is a ridiculous design flaw and should be remedied immediately.

The same is not true of positive experiences apart from the fact the mind also has no control over these either. They just happen as well but nowhere near as often. We understand some Human Minds seem to enjoy a limitless supply of these positive experiences but you probably don't have one of those minds so don't prepare for a life time of happiness because, not only is it unlikely to happen, you'll be really disappointed if you prepare for it and it doesn't happen. Sorry.

This life you are just beginning will be made easier if you just learn to cope. Please don't expect or anticipate anything good happening. If you do experience a good thing take it as a bonus rather than the normal operation of your human mind. In fact, we recommend that, in the interests of safety, you're probably best staying indoors. Phone a pizza in. The chances are no-one likes you and you were going to get fat anyway.

Stay Safe. Do Little. Change Nothing.

Sound familiar? Come on, admit it, I know you've thought like this before. You maybe even think it now. Let me tell you though, it's all rubbish and it's not how people work at all.

Here's why people don't change:

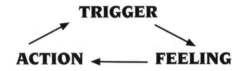

Let me explain.

People tend to believe that, when something happens in the outside world (which we will call a *trigger*), they get a *feeling* about it (that they can't control) and they will react to that feeling with some sort of *action* (that they have no real choice about). That's it. A simple model of life. Most people then believe they are destined to repeat this action until some outside factor or random occurrence changes it. They have no control over this change, it's all down to luck, divine intervention, coincidence, etc.

Here's a simple example.

Georgina sees a spider [*trigger*]. The evil thing scares the bejesus out of her [*feeling*]. She sits on the stairs afraid to go into the living room until someone gets the evil 8-legged death beast out of the house [*action*].

She has no idea why she is scared of spiders, she would tell you that she has *always* been scared of spiders and always will be and there is *nothing* in the world that can change that. It is *who she is*.

Here's another.

Simon thinks about going to meet a friend [*trigger*], all of a sudden he starts to get anxious about something or other [*feeling*], he feels sick [*feeling*]. At the last minute, he calls his friend Tony and tells him how he can't make it [*action/trigger*] and then feels guilty about calling off so late since this is now the third time he's done it [*feeling*]. He sits alone and eats a packet of chocolate biscuits [*action/trigger*] to try and remove the guilt [*feeling*]. Now he feels fat because he has just ruined his diet [*feeling*] but, when he was eating them, just for an instant, he did feel a little better [*feeling*] so now he's confused *and* guilty at the same time [*feeling*]. Confusion and guilt [*feeling*] make him want to comfort eat again [*action*] and the cycle continues!

Simon would tell you he doesn't have a problem and that he is just a 'socially anxious' person. He may even tell you that it is other people's problem because they don't understand what it is like for him and *this is who he is*.

Get the idea?

What both Simon and Georgina are actually saying is that it would, in their eyes, be easier to change the world around them than to change themselves. But they only say that because they are using the old 'instruction book'.

They have never noticed that this is not 'who they are' it's just 'something they do' and they have never been taught that changing 'what we do' is much, much easier than we tend to think it is.

If you accept this loop as a true reflection of your life, I promise you *will* stay stuck forever because it implies that you have no control over anything. Ever. Are you content to be an idle passenger in the game of life? How can you expect to change if you are just a victim of the events you experience?

We often believe we are a 'victim of circumstance'. We think we are in a fight against a life that keeps sending us trials we didn't ask for and because we spend so long fighting them we never realise the power we hold within us.

We tend to be too busy 'coping' to realise that change – permanent, lifelong, forever and ever change – is always right there within our grasp. Right now. Yes, really!

GETTING IT UNDER CONTROL

But first, before we get to change, I want to explain why sometimes we can work so hard to change something in our lives, something we really, really, want to be different and then find that it seems stuck and immovable. (Can I just add here that what you are about to read is also an approach taken by many traditional therapists and why many traditional therapies take much longer than they need to, in my opinion).

A popular approach when things aren't going our way is to try to manage and control the triggers. For example, you go to the shops and don't buy any chocolate and that means you don't need to eat it; you delete your ex's phone number and that means you don't feel an insatiable need to call or text them at 3am to gush about how much you miss them; you decide to only take trains to go on holiday because you don't want to even think about flying!

We literally and sometimes even physically force a set of rules and conditions onto our lives in a bid to keep it going in a straight line. But here's the thing, you can avoid your triggers if you want, but *nothing* is actually changing. You're just trying to avoid the feeling.

You still want the chocolate; you just don't have any and in fact, not having any is more than likely going to make you want it even more! You still have the feelings for your ex, it's just that now you can't phone them to tell them. You still get sweaty palms when you think about flying and so you still can't get to where you really want to go because of the big bloody ocean in the way!

It's a sticking plaster over a gaping wound. It will help temporarily but eventually the feelings are going to start leaking through and that's when we come to the realisation that avoiding the triggers isn't working.

So we force ourselves to do something different and move to the next part of our equation – we change our actions, i.e. the things we do and say. Fortunately, we have a built in, hardwired, tried and tested method for that.

Punishment and reward

How do you force yourself to do something you don't want to do? Whatever it is, when you don't feel like doing something, how do you motivate yourself?

Do you tell yourself how good it's going to be once it's done? Or do you take the more common approach and tell yourself that if you don't do it then you are going to get serious grief from someone, or feel really, really bad about yourself?

This is the simplest pathway to motivation – you tell yourself that, if you do the thing you need to do, either something good is going to happen or something bad is going to happen.

Punishment or Reward. Pleasure or Pain. Carrot or Stick. Call it what you like . . . it's all the same!

I meet many people who endure a four hour flight to the sunshine, sweating and white knuckled the whole way with the mantra 'I will get on the plane because, if I don't, the kids will not have a holiday.' They don't actually want to get on the plane but the pain of the kids missing out on something all their friends are doing is enough to force them into that seat and suffer hours of personal terror.

But, let's be clear, they may have survived this time but they are still terrified. That hasn't changed. Not one bit.

How many people do you know who have just enjoyed a lovely meal and then said 'I won't eat the fudge cake with chocolate chips because I have slimming club tomorrow' even though, you can tell from the look on their face, they really, really want that cake! For them, in that moment, the pain of standing on the scales and putting weight on is more than the joy of having the cake. Their motivation comes from feelings of pain.

But they still want the cake. That hasn't changed. Not one teeny, tiny chocolate chip sized little bit.

If you have ever tried this method then you will have quickly learned an important thing; you can't *force* your mind into changing!

If your mind has no reason to change what it does, no '*why*', then it will continue to 'want to' even if you stop it temporarily through the pure force of your will.

Think about your life just now. Where do you force yourself to do things? Where do you find yourself having to put 'conscious' thought into making sure you do what you want to do? Where are you battling to keep your life heading in the direction you want it to go?

You will always find it easier to do what you *want* rather than what you *should*. Until you actually *want* to change you never will, even if you and others know you really *should*.

Here's a little exercise I often use to give really useful insights into where you might be stuck and where you can make changes now.

The power of should

1. Grab a sheet of paper. Draw a line down the centre, splitting the page in two. At the top of one side write 'Should' and the other 'Want'.

2. Make a list of all the things you feel you should be doing with your life right now even if you aren't doing them. How should life be? What do other people tell you that you should be doing?

3. In that column, add in all the things you do that you know you really shouldn't be doing.

4. On the other side of the page, make a list of all the things you actually want to do. Include everything, even those things that you tell yourself will never happen!

5. Highlight or mark everything that appears in both columns.

Done? Even if you want to just do it in your head that's totally fine, you'll still get the idea.

How many matches have you found, i.e. a *should* that has a matching *want*? I'm hoping quite a few! For example 'I *should* lose weight and I *want* to lose weight', or 'I *should* organise my time better and I *want* to organise my time better'.

These are definitely good news for you but it's the others are usually far more revealing!

Because, if a *should* doesn't have a corresponding *want*, we have to ask why not? Is there a reason for it not being there and is that reason positive and empowering or negative and potentially destructive?

A positive reason might be when you resist living by someone else's rules or expectations. Some examples I have heard before, 'I should be married but I don't want to be married', 'I should go to the gym but I don't want to go to the gym' or 'I should leave, but I don't want to leave.

If you follow someone else's 'shoulds' I promise you will end up living someone else's version of your life. And that's bad news! It is your life to live and, as long as you aren't deliberately hurting yourself or anyone else, you do what ever the hell you *want* with it. Not what others say you 'should'.

However, in understanding positive reasons, it also becomes more apparent from where the negative reasons come.

What about those unsupported 'shoulds' where you are hurting yourself or someone else and still you continue to do it? Maybe you are overweight, a smoker, drinking too much, working too much, staying in a relationship that really doesn't serve you and never will. Wanting these things to stop are all perfect examples of good 'shoulds'! Then the obvious question becomes . . . if you should, why don't you want to?

I remember when I was a smoker I tried to use willpower to give up many times. It was absolute torture because although I knew I *should* give up, my deeper emotional mind wasn't ready. I simply didn't want to.

Basically, I was unconsciously aware that I enjoyed more from smoking than I would if it were taken away. I never had a chance. The wee voice in my head would be there, from the very first morning of all my designated 'Giving Up Days', telling me how much I needed it, how much I wanted it.

Cravings made my mind feel like it was full of marshmallow, my muscles felt tired, heavy and sore. I'd be tired and moody and I'd try and fight it but, if I was being honest, all I could focus my attention on was the niggling certainty that sooner or later I would give in. In an odd way, I liked that feeling because it meant that this horrible 'giving up' sensation and cravings weren't going to last forever. It was an escape from my 'should'.

Of course, I claimed 'next time it will be different' but, to be honest, the longest I ever lasted was about three days. That is until I gave up completely . . . of which more later.

The simple fact is that it is difficult, perhaps even verging on impossible, simply to change by forcing yourself to do something different. If you have to force yourself, you'll just end up with your 'wants' overcoming your 'shoulds'. For example:

- Do you fight and struggle to control your eating?

- Do you need to drag yourself out of bed every morning to go to work and then hate it once you're there?

- Do you put a big, brave face on in certain situations and hide how you really feel inside?

- Do you do some things simply because that's what you've always done or because they have a positive influence on your life?

- Do you find yourself tired all the time because you are working ridiculously hard just to keep your emotions together?

Controlling our behaviour is hard work because our mind is one of the strongest muscles in our body and when it wants something you are going to need a ridiculous amount of will power to keep it quiet.

When you think about it, your mind is pulling you one way by giving you an emotional direction and then you have to fight to pull it in another direction using just your willpower.

It is a 24hr, 7 days a week, 365 days a year tug of war between the emotional you and the rational you.

And here's the thing. . . . Emotional will ALWAYS win!!

If you don't have an emotional reason to stop something then you can never stop, can you? If you stop fighting and controlling it with all that willpower, then that emotional 'thing' just comes spilling out all over the place and you can't do anything to stop it. If those emotional reasons have not been found then you need non-stop effort. You *need* to keep tugging tightly on that emotional rope, even when you're losing, or the whole thing will fall to bits.

And do you want to know what makes this even worse?

Every time your willpower loses that game of tug of war it weakens slightly and loses a little bit of its strength. The next time you try to use that willpower it will be nowhere near as strong and, even though you want it more than anything, it seems like the tank is empty and you have less to give.

You are training your willpower muscles to be soft and floppy rather than strong and tight. It is possible to win, but the battle will leave you drained.

Woohoo! Check me out. Mr. Positive! Are you feeling good about yourself yet? Well the good news is that it's not all doom and gloom and I really want you to understand one key point. . . .

**If you want to win the battle
you need to change the way you think.**

Read that line again. Go on, just for me. . . .

THE FLIP SIDE

Before I tell you more about that, it's also important to understand that sometimes we just *need* to do something.

Isn't it true that the best things in life come from that moment when we do something even when we are scared, when we say something that needs to be said even though we don't know what response we will get, when we act even though we have no idea of the outcome? It's these moments that define you because it's in these moments that you push your mind to do something different.

Because the mind works in patterns, it's easy to get stuck, doing the same thing and staying within the boundaries of what is 'normal' and 'comfortable'. Doing 'normal' and 'comfortable' is not how we change. Change happens when we go beyond these boundaries.

Remember I said earlier that we are all here because some brave cave dweller asked something along the lines of 'hey, what do you think is over there?' and went to explore, leaving 'normal' and 'comfortable' behind.

When we stretch our boundaries, pushing them a little further than they want to go, the boundaries will change and with enough of a push, will change permanently.

Again, think of your mind like a muscle. If you can manage just one more press up, move one second faster, put in one extra repetition on the weights, your muscles *will* get stronger.

How many special things have you experienced in life that are the direct result of doing something you didn't think you could possibly do? And how many of those special things do you now think you could easily do again?

Have you ever had an extreme experience? You know like walking over fire, walking on broken glass, a parachute jump, bungee jump or something similar? When we take these challenges it is never about the jump or the walk or whatever. What is most important to learn is that when we put our minds to it and go for it, we can do amazing things, even when we don't think we can.

Just like a muscle, every time you do something new, every time you push your mind just a wee bit further than it wants to go, every time you make yourself uncomfortable and push your boundaries, your mind gets stronger.

I know that if I help someone push their boundaries and walk a firewalk, a barefoot march over 12 feet of burning coals, then I have helped them make their mind stronger. What will they be capable of next time life throws them a challenge?

So ask yourself, where have you faced uncertainty, met the challenge head on and just gone for it, in the process, making yourself and your mind that little bit stronger? And have you ever taken the time to actually give yourself the credit you deserve for doing it?

Do this next task in your head or on paper and allow yourself to appreciate some of the special things you've done.

Hidden strengths

1. Think about your whole life just now and name three amazing things you told yourself you couldn't do or wouldn't do, that you have now done? These things don't have to be huge life changing events – they may be relatively modest achievements that have extra special meaning to you.

2. If you could go back and visit a younger version of yourself who said these things would never, ever happen, what would you say to them, now you have achieved them, that would give them more self belief?

3. What would this younger version of yourself think of you now, having achieved these amazing things?

If you repeat this exercise often, it will help you take pride in your achievements. Ignore anyone who reminds you that pride is a 'sin'. I'm pretty sure that was a heavenly administrative mistake anyway!

Take a moment to reflect on what we have learned here – whatever that wee voice in your head might tell you, you are more than you think you are and capable of more than you realise.

MENTAL AEROBICS

So what's the difference?

Why is it that sometimes controlling our behaviour is about will power and holding ourselves together and other times it's about pushing forward and making ourselves awesome?

For example, if I decide to eat a whole packet of chocolate biscuits tonight, even though I tell myself I shouldn't, can I then tell myself that I have pushed my boundaries and take pride in my bravery for taking on such a significant challenge?

Well of course not!!

I've just stretched the muscle the wrong way. I've suggested to myself that I can eat a whole packet of chocolate biscuits. Why would that be a good thing? Next I'll want to push more boundaries and try two packs!

We have to ask ourselves if we are pushing and stretching our mind in the right direction, because any muscle will become stronger in the direction you push it.

In short, forcing our negative actions to feel positive only tends to work *short term*. Trying to fight our feelings and change through willpower alone is tiring, often futile, and weakens our behavioural 'muscles' to the point we will probably just give in.

And not only that, if you choose to rely on willpower, it is almost guaranteed that your battle will be long and the losses significant. So, in most cases, as time goes on and the losses mount up, we give up and blame feelings for our inability to change. 'It isn't my fault, it's just the feelings I get.'

Hmmmm, or is it?

ONE SIMPLE FIX, 100% GUARANTEED

If we've removed all our triggers and failed to control our actions then we arrive at the next logical step. We look to change the way we feel. Have you ever thought, 'maybe, just maybe, if I can control my feelings, life will be different?'

On a daily basis, we are bombarded with pressure to control our feelings:

- **Drink this coffee** (or you'll **feel** tired).

- **Buy this car** (or you won't **feel** safe/sexy/attractive).

- **Wear this perfume** (or you wont **feel** beautiful/glamorous/as good as everyone else).

- **Go on this diet** (or you'll **feel** unhappy).

We watch TV shows for escapism, we eat for comfort, we drink for stress relief, we take medicine for emotional support . . . we live life merely managing our feelings rather than enjoying a life filled with rich and varied emotions.

Why??

To begin with, most people believe that changing their feelings is really, really hard. If you are one of the 'most people' (and almost everyone reading this, including me, will be one of the 'most people') I would guess that you find yourself, some of the time at least, at the mercy of your circumstances. Outside events trigger certain emotions and you develop a coping strategy to deal with them. A simple example is *comfort* (emotion) *eating* (coping strategy). The clue is in the name and the key question to any comfort eater is one that is too rarely asked – from what are they seeking comfort?

Taking a moment to reflect on your own coping strategies you may notice that many of them have a simpler name;

Medication

Think about it, we spend a lot of time (and money) relying on external 'stuff' to help us feel better. Coffee, alcohol, smoking, shopping, drugs, TV, food, sex, attention, work, chaos, car, phone, diet, clothes, club, whatever. Every single one is a form of medication.

Now, using the word in this context, it's important to know that some of our 'medication' can be fun and is, sometimes, completely necessary. It simply depends on why you are 'taking' it.

My wife says I spend more on clothes than she does, which may or may not be true – I do love shopping. For example, before a new training course starts, I like to buy something new to wear on day one if I can because it gives me a wee special feeling standing in front of the group.

Is that medication? Well, yes. I suppose it is.

It changes how I feel and gives me a lift for that important first day of a course, so it definitely fits our definition of medication. But do I need therapy for it? No, of course not, because there is a difference between 'good' medication and 'bad' medication.

Many of us have these medications – sport, shopping, friends, music, films, TV, gaming, dancing, etc. And this is the difference . . . we don't *need* them, we choose to have them because they enrich our lives and make us feel good.

I can't always get to the shops before a course begins but I still stand up there on day one and deliver the same course in the same way. A new purchase is not essential, it's just something I enjoy when and if I can. I'm sure you feel the same about many things you enjoy. Like me, you probably have many things you enjoy but that you can live perfectly well without. It's not the end of the world if you don't have your favourite shower gel. If your best friend can't meet you at the weekend (oh yes, people can be medication too!) you'll be disappointed but maybe rearrange for the week after and still look forward to seeing him/her then. An early night could be just what you need anyway. . . .

But then again, are there medications that you can't live without? Could you live without coffee, cigarettes, Facebook, credit cards, a phone? Take a moment to think about what you have in your life that you really *need*. Not that you just want it, you actually *need* it and if you can't get it your life may very well be thrown into crisis!

Difficult isn't it?

Often it's not until we are forced to live without something that we realise how much we really *need* it.

Let's consider an example. I meet many teenagers these days that are hooked on energy drinks. They consume a large amount of these and often tell me that they don't know how they'd function without the bizarrely flavoured caffeine and sugar brew. One teenager recently described it to me as his 'lifeblood'. I resisted the temptation to patiently explain that their actual lifeblood is 'blood' and it does a grand job without huge quantities of sugar and caffeine! Frighteningly, many teenagers become anxious without access to these drinks and believe they have difficulty remembering information and studying.

How many people do you know that would say the same about coffee or tea? I met a client recently who told me that he drinks about ten cups of coffee a day. In fact, in his words 'the day can't start until I have my morning cup'. For many, many people caffeine is medication. Socially acceptable, even socially expected it may be, but it is still a drug that people say they *need* to be able to feel the way they want to feel.

And that is a problem. . . .

When we get an emotion we don't like, we first of all hope it will just go away. We try and ignore it, hoping that it will just pass. Maybe we're imagining it. Maybe it will just disappear.

But then, if it doesn't disappear, we find a dark corner of our mind, build a big strong box, chuck the emotion in and then close it all up as quickly as we can. But that doesn't work for every feeling. Some feelings are tenacious and will simply keep on reappearing. No matter how often we try to put them in the box, they keep on coming back to hurt us!

It's usually at this point we look for medication to help, anything that will help us numb/hide/distract from that feeling that won't stay gone. As we've seen, that medication might be chocolate, wine, sex, drugs, work in fact anything at all that will take us into a different feeling quickly and let us forget that other feeling, even briefly.

And, once we've found a medicine that works, we want to take it every time that feeling appears. It becomes a pattern.

If, after a period of time, our usual medication loses its potency and stops working as well as it used to, we will find (or be prescribed) a stronger one or simply take more and more until we get the feeling we believe we need.

This might all sound very dramatic but if you look around there are so many of us doing this that we just take it for granted.

For example, we have grown to be a society that accepts stress as a natural part of living and we also accept all the forms of medication the world offers us to cope with it. And patterns of medication are where addictions come from. People don't become addicted to things, they become addicted to the feelings the things give them. There are no addictive personalities, there are only people who have lost touch with how to feel without outside help.

Luckily, as we are about to discover, it doesn't have to be this way! Stress, sadness, anger, fear and guilt may well have become natural parts of modern life but they are not necessarily natural parts of modern *living*.

Here's another quick test you can do either in your head or in your notebook that will quickly reveal your 'good' and 'bad' medications.

Clearing out your pharmacy

1. What do you tell yourself you *cannot* live without in your life?

2. What things do you do or have regularly that truly enrich your life and feel like a positive choice every time you experience them?

3. If you were to *stop* doing two things right now that would make a significant difference to your life what would they be?

4. What feelings would you no longer have after stopping these two things, e.g. relaxation, excitement etc?

5. If you were to *start* doing two things right now that would make a significant difference to your life what would they be?

6. What feelings would doing these two things regularly from now on give you?

7. What long term difference would it make to your life now if you took these actions *today*?

Interesting exercise isn't it? If I had to guess, I'd say you will have either discovered things you have to change (new entries for your *want* and *should* lists) or you will realise that actually things are going pretty good right now! Either way, you're winning.

Most of us will have found at least one thing we want to change and, I would expect, will have had the next logical thought – 'yeah, but how the hell do I do it?'

Well, here's the good news . . . listen carefully. . . .

Every resource and ability you need to change every feeling you have is inside you right now.

Now read that again. Out loud if you can do it without attracting too much attention. It really is true but because we either don't realise or don't believe it, we spend our time forcing ourselves to do things we don't want to do and then spend more time (and often money) medicating the feelings that result from forcing ourselves to do those things we didn't want to do in the first place! Is that not completely ridiculous?

You don't need medication to change how you feel. You were born with all the knowledge and power you need to change your feelings. So many of us give up that power because we think it is reserved for special people. People who are not like us. People who make life look so damn easy.

Why is it that some people seem to manage their feelings so easily and manage to deal with the pressure and stresses of life without using medications?

THE SECRET, THE KEY, THE MISSING LINK

Well, I'm really sorry to have to tell you this but they are just special and you're not. You were obviously born one of life's victims and desperately lack the skills and knowledge needed to change. Obviously that's disappointing, but there is also good news. You have somehow managed to survive this long. Which is nice. Well done. But since you're not already like the happy, special, chosen people, then you may as well just accept that your life is screwed!! I apologise for any inconvenience this may cause and wish you well as you struggle through whatever semblance of life you have left. . . .

. . . . .

Ok, I'm just kidding . . . sorry if I freaked you out!

We all have the ability to change, no one is special. You have the same working parts as everyone else on this planet, it's just that no-one has ever shown you how to use them in the right way.

The secret to making life easy (or at least easier) is to look *behind* the feelings and ask yourself 'what makes me feel?'. Then ask 'what would happen if I change the cause rather than the effect?'

I always remember an early teacher of mine using a metaphor which asked 'how many sticks of dynamite does it take to bring down a 100ft arched bridge made of stone?'[1]

The answer is just one, if you put it in the right place. And that, very simply, is the secret of change.

It only takes seconds to change anything in life. The tricky bit is finding where to put your stick of dynamite.

One of the reasons we find it difficult to change is because believing we are at the mercy of our circumstances keeps us stuck. It places all the power outside of our control. Here's our loop again.

---

[1] Engineers . . . no need to write in, it's a metaphor!

That's why we go looking for external medication to help. If the cause is outside us then surely the cure must be outside too, right? But it's not. It's right there in front of us. We even talk about it, we tell people about it and we don't even realise we're doing it.

When I tried to give up smoking all those years ago, straining my willpower to get me through the 'dark days' of cravings and desperation for a cigarette there were two constants – the belief that I still wanted to smoke and the thought 'I want a cigarette now'. I now realise that this *thought* was the reason I never succeeded.

When you walk past the chocolate biscuits in the supermarket, refusing to buy them in a defiant show of strength and courage, you congratulate yourself for your bravery in the face of a whole aisle of chocolatey deliciousness. But then, later that evening not long after dinner, comes that thought . . . the *thought* 'I want some chocolate'.

When you have survived the flight over there by gritting your teeth, holding back the tears and seeing it through for the family, there is still one thing that will cause you to shake and drink copious amounts of gin in the departure lounge for the flight home. The *thought* 'What if this plane crashes?'

You see?

You are not truly affected by your circumstances. You are affected by your *thoughts about* those circumstances.

When I finally gave up cigarettes once and for all, it was by changing the *thought* that smoking was helping me in any way whatsoever. The very second I changed the way I thought about smoking and realised that for everything I thought I was gaining from smoking I was losing much, much more, it was easy to just stop. I don't like losing things!

I thought smoking made me look cool. That was the thought I had when I started smoking at 17 and that was the thought I needed to change at 31 when I finally stopped. Because I changed the *thought*, I changed the *feeling* associated with that thought. And because I changed the feeling, my actions changed.

It was amazing! And instant.

But still I have a clear memory of actually pushing myself to try and start again! Now my willpower seemed to be pushing me into smoking!

Why would my mind want to hijack one of my greatest triumphs?

Because I felt as if I was losing something by not smoking! I saw other people smoking and I wanted to be part of their group. Luckily for me, I couldn't! Trust me, I actually tried! The last cigarette that touched my lips was in 2004 on holiday in South Wales. I had one puff and there were absolutely no good feelings with it. No enjoyment, no calming affect, just a horrible taste, a feeling of regret and a deep awareness that the whole process was a totally pointless act. Just holding the cigarette felt alien and strange.

I have never smoked since.

**Your thoughts make you
and your thoughts change you.**

When people change and make life seem effortless, their success is often due to simply forcing themselves to do something different. They don't just look for a cuddle and someone to tell them it will all be OK (although they might not refuse one if it is offered). They change the way they think about the world and, when they do that, they gain the power to change everything.

Yes . . . everything.

Chapter 1 *in a nutshell*:

- Your mind is a logical, pattern creation device and not as crazy as it may seem.

- We find it difficult to change because hiding from our triggers, controlling our actions and medicating our feelings produce short term results.

- Buried emotions aren't going anywhere and will leak out. Talk about them – one of the best medications is to release them.

- There is no need for magic potions or gurus. Every resource and ability you need to change every feeling you have, is inside you right now. Trust yourself.

- Your thoughts make you and your thoughts can change you.

The big, fat, greasy slob – revisited

You see, perception is everything. Reality is of no concern to our minds. Have you ever woken up, looked at yourself in the mirror, felt bloated and out of shape then two hours later after coming back from the gym, looked at yourself again and was sure you'd lost weight? Perception is everything.

It didn't take long to realise that Jodie's problem wasn't really deep, dark depression as she had initially thought. In fact, as she had explained on the phone, her life was largely happy and she had some very special people in it. Depressive feelings tend to be darkly pervasive, allowing very little light through. Jodie's life was largely shiny and bright. I knew almost instantly this wasn't depression.

However, Jodie was experiencing a really severe anxiety reaction about her appearance. Every negative thing she could identify in her life came down to how she looked including her marriage where, for example, she believed she was too ugly to deserve her husband and she was ruining his life because he could and should have someone much better looking than her. Her sisters were perfect and she was 'a dog'. She was too tall, too fat, her eyes were the wrong colour, her hips were too big, her hair wasn't blonde and her boobs were too small. That is only a small sample from her list of faults!

Everything came down to how she looked.

Doctors had given her pills, lots of people had told her to stop being silly, her husband was eternally patient, reassuring and loving but no one had ever actually taken the time to talk to her for long enough to realise that she wasn't depressed. But she did need to change her perception of herself and I was confident that it wouldn't even take very long.

When you begin teaching people how easy it is to work with their mind, they can make incredible changes happen incredibly quickly (never subscribe to the notion that change has to take years. It just takes effort and focus).

Jodie accepted almost immediately that she wasn't depressed. My explanation of what was really going on was enough to change that thought. Then we could start working with what really needed to change and we got amazing results.

By taking that step beyond her feelings to discover where they came from, we had perfectly placed our stick of dynamite. In less than two sessions, Jodie started to see things differently and live her life again.

Now, Jodie is very happy, still madly in love, has been promoted to a job she loves even more than the old one and now enjoys getting dressed up every chance she can get. She still sometimes wishes her hair was blonde and apparently she could still do with losing a 'couple of pounds' but, for the most part, she is happy with herself and her life is now, to use her own word, 'amazing'.

One of the most powerful changes you can ever make is to accept and appreciate yourself. Until you do, no one else can.

Meeting my match

Madison is a fascinating girl. When I first met her she was only 13 and our initial work together was all about controlling her temper, something she readily admitted could easily get out of control.

An important and sometimes tricky part of working with teenagers is to get on well with them – with Madison, this was actually very easy. We hit it off immediately and dealt with the anger relatively quickly but it was obvious to me something else was going on. For a 13 year old she had the most incredible imagination, which was clear from her poetry and stories, though the subject matter for these creative outlets was pretty dark. She also had an amazing knack for deflecting and diverting conversations away from the matter at hand, especially when they were potentially becoming too emotional. To an experienced coach, this is a big red flag indicating something hiding in there that the person wants you to be deflected away from.

At first I wasn't sure what it was that she was hiding. Each time I asked her directly, I had to call her out on the bizarre tangents to which she then tried to take the conversation. At age 13 she hadn't quite enough experience nor had she developed the strategies to completely hide the fact that there was something serious lurking under the surface. She gave it a pretty good shot though and her tactics became more and more extreme! For example, a common reaction to my probing her emotions and state of mind was for her to slide off the chair and onto the floor, claiming that she couldn't get up!

I talked to her mum frequently about the challenges of unravelling Madison's emotions – we needed to find a way that would allow Madison to feel comfortable exploring her emotions, while not actually realising that she was exploring her emotions! Between her mum and I, we hatched a cunning plan to use Madison's stories, poetry and fantasies as a way in to unlock the deeper emotional issues hidden beneath.

Like others whose stories you will discover as you read on, Madison invented imaginary characters that she used to actively channel her emotions. I had to keep reminding myself that these characters, about whom she spoke in such great detail, were not actually real. They were simply ways for her to process the emotions that she had repressed when her older sister experienced a period of self harm. She had confided in Madison and asked her to keep it a secret – that secret was a big burden for a little girl only 11 years old at the time.

You see, secret emotions have nowhere to go. The more we try to hide them, ignore them and suppress them, the more the emotions need an outlet – the conflict can be unbearable and this is exactly what Madison was experiencing.

Her emotions found their outlet in her dark stories, poetry and fictional social media accounts where she played out real emotions through characters with elaborate back stories. Like a secret cry for help to the outside world, she would write messages such as 'why can no-one see me, am I invisible?' on her body in felt tip pen, then be careful to ensure they were in places no-one would see. All the signs were clearly laid out, almost inviting me to help, I just couldn't seem to guide Madison towards making her breakthrough.

If I'm being honest, after several sessions, I was becoming concerned that, despite all my efforts, techniques, training, patience and ninja-like conversational stealth, I just wasn't getting through. There was an amazing young woman in there fighting to be free from the pain and I was really struggling to find a way to help her.

Then one sunny afternoon in late spring, I asked Madison a question I had never asked her before and the change was almost instantaneous.

2

Blowing bubbles

Have you ever, in a fleeting moment of summertime whimsy, taken a big wedge of lemon and presented it to a young child on the pretence that your gift is some sort of sweet treat? Not that I am suggesting you play such an evil trick on any unsuspecting child, but there is a strange delight in watching as their face contorts as they experience the unexpected sour taste for the first time!

Think about it now. Try to remember the first time you ever tasted lemon. How strong was the flavour? Did it hit you all at once or was more gradual? If you can't remember the first time, try thinking about the most recent time instead. The distinctive lemony smell, the acidy tartness that makes you want to suck your cheeks in, the lingering aftertaste – try to really immerse yourself in everything lemon.

Now, this will be more powerful for some than others but, as you think about the lemon, is your mouth watering?

Well, that's a bit odd isn't it . . .? There is obviously no lemon yet your body responds as if there is. This little experiment demonstrates one of the fundamental workings of the mind.

You only need to *think* about a lemon (or anything else for that matter) and your mind and body will respond *as if* it was real, producing effects similar to those that would be experienced in the presence of the real stimulus.

And in that lemon-flavoured nutshell is the secret to every emotion you will ever feel in your life . . . your mind does not know the difference between something that is real and something that is imagined. It will respond the same way to both.

This is very, very important. It's so important, in fact, I'm not only going to say it again but I'm also going to give it a line all to itself. . . .

Your mind does *not* know the difference between something that is real and something that is imagined.

When a picture of something pops onto the wee movie screen inside your head, your mind unconsciously triggers the appropriate emotional and physical responses regardless of whether the stimulus is right in front of you in real life or simply something you've made up.

It's important to realise that your mind only pays attention to what is playing on your movie screen even though what is playing may have nothing to do with the reality of the world around you or your circumstances within that world. Now that may not make a lot of sense just now, but just file it away and we'll come back to it later.

So why is this important? Am I suggesting you can change your life simply by thinking of lemons? Do I intend to treat all modern mental health issues with my citrus-based imagination game? Well, no, but think of it like this . . . if our unconscious mind only perceives our reality on the inside, what would happen if we replace the lemon with something else on the screen?

Think of strawberries. Does that have the same effect? Think about your favourite childhood meal. Does that cause your mouth to water or does it cause other feelings to appear? What if this technique were to be applied to your life.

- What if, rather than playing a movie featuring an event or memory that makes you feel happy and grateful, you play a movie about a silly mistake that left you feeling useless and a failure?

- What if, rather than looking forward to arriving on a sunny beach somewhere, you are playing a movie about your plane crashing into the sea?

- What if, rather than thinking about what you are going to do later that evening to relax and unwind after a long day, all you play inside your mind are images of chocolate biscuits and cigarettes?

Understanding this concept is so important for your own personal change journey that I'm going to repeat myself one more time for effect. In italics!

> *Your mind does not know the difference between something that is real and something that is imagined.*

It doesn't matter if it's a lemon, a memory of the happiest day of your life or a horrible memory you'd rather forget, your thoughts (i.e. the pictures and movies on your screen) cause you to respond by feeling. These thoughts will override your reality and

you will feel whatever you think.

If you think lemon, you will respond as if the lemon is real. If you think plane crash, you will respond as if it is real. If you think 'I'm not good enough', you will respond as if you are not good enough. It is also important to know this works both ways, if you think 'I am truly loved and cared for', you will feel that gorgeous glow of love inside, feel wanted and cared for and your day will be just a little more awesome.

This is our missing link from Chapter 1, this is the secret to living happy. Our thoughts are the origin of all of our feelings. Our diagram should actually look like this:

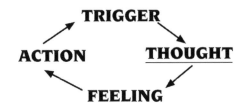

Now take a deep breath and you might want to sit down for this bit. If you are a fan of the Matrix movies, imagine this in the voice of Morpheus. . . .

You will never 'touch' reality. You are never truly seeing or hearing the world as it is because nothing that you are currently experiencing is actually real.

Well, at least not in the way you currently understand 'real'.

Everything you currently see, everything you currently hear, everything you are currently feeling, tasting and smelling is being filtered by your mind. You are actually experiencing a secondary reality, filtered through a lifetime of experience and learning. Your current experience is only a *version* of reality. To be even more precise, your current experience is only *your* version of reality.

Pretty mind-blowing isn't it?

There is not one other person anywhere experiencing the world in exactly the same way you are right now. There has never been anyone like you before and there never, ever will be again.

Every single experience you are surrounded by, every sound you have ever heard and will ever hear, every single thing you have seen or will ever see, and every sensation and emotion that you have experienced and are yet to experience, are all absolutely and totally unique to you. No-one will ever repeat them or experience them in the same way. Your version of this world is a one off event as unique as a fingerprint or a snowflake.

Now, to keep your version of the world familiar and comfortable, your mind has to act like a filter; changing and twisting your reality to make it match what you expect to see, hear and feel. In doing that, it produces a lifetime of unique experiences.

I often describe that filter like living inside a bubble that alters and interprets our reality in various ways to make it fit our expectations.

As an example, imagine a football match that has just come to an end.

After a fantastic game, both sets of supporters leave the stadium and, if we could listen to a sample of the conversations on each side, they would be very similar. Both are talking about how their team played brilliantly, how the other team were useless and played dirty and how the referee gave their team no decisions at all and was obviously biased towards the opponents.

So, both sets of fans can claim refereeing bias while also claiming their team played exciting and skillful football and the other team played like a bunch of amateurs. How can that be? I mean, who's right?

Well, you could argue that neither are. Or perhaps they both are. Both sets of fans have witnessed the same game but filtered through their 'bubble'. Every individual at the game witnessed his or her own perception of it – they only saw their *own version* of the game. And there could be any number of versions for any number of people.

For example, what would happen if we asked the referee how the game went?
Or a supporter of a third team watching as a neutral?
Or the manager of a team hoping for a particular result because it helped his team?
Or someone who doesn't know the rules of the game?

Each of these reports would be different yet every one would also be more or less accurate. The cold hard facts of the game (score, fouls, cautions, etc) don't actually matter, only how they are perceived by the viewers.

So let's take that one step further. What if the cold hard facts of *any* experience don't actually matter and all that matters about any experience is how the person experiencing it perceives it. This is how vital perception is to any event and, when you consider any experience from a different 'angle', everything seems different.

Your experience of *any* event depends entirely on your perception of it – a set of facts filtered by your 'bubble' to form *your* reality.

If this is true, then it must be possible to change your reality by simply changing your thinking. Let's test that.

If you think you lack confidence in a particular area of your life, what is it that you specifically think about that area of life that takes your confidence away?

If you don't like your job/relationship/other area of your life right now, what is it that you think that stops you changing it?

And when you are being the most amazing version of you, what is it that you think that allows you to let it all out and show it all off?

As you'll remember from earlier, your thoughts alter your reality and if you change a thought, you will change a feeling. And that means, if you change a feeling, you will change the action that you take.

Thought = Feeling = Action

So, go ahead and change your thoughts. No more battling with willpower. No more addictive medications. Sounds easy doesn't it? But the question then becomes *how* do you change your thoughts?

Well, I'm glad you asked. . . .

LIMITATIONS OF EXPERIENCE

Have you ever been on a long car journey and found yourself bored by the music on your usual radio station? Since you have no idea what else is on, you just set your radio to 'scan' and let it search through the stations looking for something that catches your ear.

You find yourself listening to little bits of lots of stuff, briefly singing along to Mariah Carey, listening to random country songs with weird titles like 'I Fell In A Pile Of You And Got Love All Over Me' and 'I Gave Her My Heart And A Diamond And She Clubbed Me With A Spade',[1] and, for at least three minutes longer than you mean to, you listen to a very heated debate on welfare reform before you snap out of it and scan again. You can go on like this for hours, catching little bits of station after station, music, chat, comedy, game shows, debate, news, travel, sport, a near endless choice and all of it comes from just three bands – LW, AM and FM.

Now, you aren't even aware that you are surrounded by this information all the time. Wherever you are just now you are surrounded by potential information. You could have walked right through the classic 'My Poppa Was With Custer When He Stood On That There Hill'[1] and the latest breaking news could be passing right through your body right now without you even noticing. You are currently existing in radio soup and you don't even realise.

But, with the right equipment, tuned to the right frequency, you can hear it all easily. When you push the power button on your radio, that doesn't switch the signal on. The signal is always there. You just need to choose to listen.

We are surrounded by a huge amount of potential information simply waiting for us to notice it and our 'bubble' is always scanning. So if we set it to the right frequency, we can change the way we experience this information. And the good news is that we don't just have three bands – we have five!

---

[1] These really are genuine titles!

This next exercise is a little thought experiment to look at what happens when you start 're-tuning' your bubble. Let's start the experiment now, get your bubble tuned in, then we'll come back later in the book and wrap it up. Pay close attention – there may be a test!

Magic numbers

Starting now, I want you to notice something for me. You don't have to write anything down, just simply put something in your mind and leave it there.

I remember being a teenager and being told that there was a particular number that had a kind of hidden, universal meaning. I was told it had connections to physics, nature, quantum theory even the Illuminati and that the number would crop up in the most unexpected places.

Bizarrely, once I started looking for it I found this to be true and I invite you to see this in action for yourself. From now until you finish reading this book, all you have to do is look out for this mystical number. I want you to tune yourself in to it and notice how often it crops up in car registrations, conversations, websites, road signs, television programs [especially Star Trek!] and a myriad of other places in your world.

The number is **23** and I promise you, it's everywhere. Sometimes it proudly stands on it's own, other times it's a wee bit sneaky and hides in prices (£2.30), postcodes (G2 3PH), times (2.39pm), phone numbers, all manner of places. Also listen for it cropping up in conversation.

We'll come back a bit later and explain more. Oh, and while you are at it, you should watch out for the woman in the red shoes. You'll know her when you see her. . . .

The mind receives info through five 'bands', better known as the senses – sight, sound, sensation/touch, smell and taste.[2]

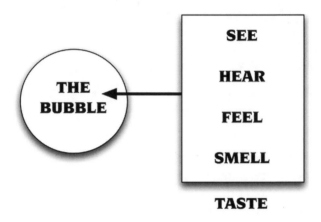

In every waking minute of your life you are unconsciously receiving a constant stream of information through four of these senses and storing it for future use, in what we call *memories*. Taste is the odd one out as that spends most of its time in background mode waiting until it is needed.

No matter where you are and no matter what you are doing right now, you are seeing, hearing, feeling and smelling the world around you but you are not consciously aware of most of the information being received. In fact, if it were even possible for you to be consciously aware of all the information your senses are receiving right at this very second, you would be completely overwhelmed in seconds and probably go a little bit mad!

---

[2] I've heard it suggested that we actually have 30+ senses. Maybe that's right, maybe it's not. I'm sticking with five for now.

So to help you navigate the world, your bubble (aka unconscious mind) deciphers and decodes the information before it decides which bits you will receive. It does all it can to keep your world 'normal', i.e. how you expect it to be, within normal parameters, the way it *should* be. And to be honest it does a pretty good job of this most of the time, using a number of key techniques of which you are not consciously aware.

WHAT DID YOU SAY?

The first technique your mind uses to help you make sense of 'normal' life is to just plain *ignore* huge chunks of the information that surrounds you!

The famous Scottish psychologist R.D. Laing said,

> "The range of what we think and do is limited by what we fail to notice. And because we fail to notice that we fail to notice, there is little we can do to change; until we notice how failing to notice shapes our thoughts and deeds."[3]

On first reading, as with much of Laing's written work, this seems to make no sense at all, but go back and read it a couple more times. . . . The more you read it the more you see he is actually making a great deal of sense. Let me use a metaphor to explain.

Some animals are born in a cage. Some may argue that, because the animal will never know that anything more than its cage exists and has nothing to compare to its limited existence, it cannot possibly be unhappy.

---

[3] Attributed to Lang RD. In: Seymour JL, Crain MA, Crockett JV. *Educating Christians*, 1993. p. 53.

Now I don't necessarily mean a literal cage here – for example, an elephant born in the circus is unaware of the open plains and cannot miss the freedom of vast empty space, a chimpanzee born in a zoo is unaware of the jungle so it never knows there are endless tree tops it will never climb. Because they have never known and are not aware of anything other than what they have, they will never strive for more. Likewise, a goldfish is unaware of the ocean so it believes swimming in circles is all there is and has no perception that their world is, or can be, any different to how it is now.

So let me ask, how much like that goldfish are you? Are you limited by what you fail to notice?

I have met many people who believe they are never paid compliments or praised for their actions when, in actual fact, they are complimented and praised all the time. It's just that, when it happens, they don't know how to accept the compliment so they reject it and, in doing so, their mind simply 'deletes' the compliment from existence. By never accepting a compliment it becomes easy to pretend compliments never happen.

All it takes for us to stop ignoring what is happening around us is to stop and notice what is happening around us. Problem solved!! And it's actually pretty easy to do.

Take a little time to concentrate on this next exercise. Just a few minutes of focused thought can produce amazing rewards. Have a go either in your head or on paper and let's see what you find.

Noticing the unnoticed

1. If you were to tell me three positive things about you as a person that no one else knows, what would they be?

2. If I was to ask your best friends or family about the three most positive aspects of you, what would they say?

3. If you could step back from your life right now and see it all at once, what is the single most positive thing you would notice that you have never noticed before?

This short set of questions is one that is useful to ask yourself often. Did you find it easier to answer question 2 than 1 or 3? Did you find it hard to answer them all? If so, then you need to go back and do the exercise again! What are you failing to notice? Stop. Think. Focus. Then try the questions again.

Too many of us live our lives in a 'cage'. What we often fail to notice is that the cage is only as real as the imaginary lemon that made our mouths water at the top of the chapter . . . it only exists in our mind. Sometimes we need to step back to get the full perspective, to begin to notice what we are failing to notice.

For instance, let me set you a very simple yet potentially difficult challenge. Let's return to the concept of accepting compliments.

Next time you are paid a compliment or given a gift, no matter how big or small, I want you to accept it with a simple and sincere 'thank you'. That's it. You are allowed *no* qualifying statements about how they shouldn't have or how they are just saying that. No telling them they are mistaken or wrong. No need to give them a compliment back. Just respond with that simple and sincere 'thank you' and then move on.

Many people, especially the famously reserved British, feel much more comfortable [aka 'normal'] believing they aren't attractive, clever, kind or special and will attempt to ignore any compliment by telling the giver all the ways in which they are wrong.

'No, no, it's just something I threw on'.
'You shouldn't have, it's no big deal'.
'I think I just got lucky'.
'Oh no, I'm not special at all'.
'I didn't really do that great job, it was really someone else'.

Do you do this? Perhaps you don't want to seem big headed or vain or perhaps it's that you really don't believe what the person is trying to tell you, but when you reject or deflect a compliment you restrict yourself. You keep yourself small. You deny yourself happiness. You refuse to notice what you have failed to notice and you keep yourself locked in a cage.

By responding 'thank you' to each and every compliment you are now given, I am asking you to force your mind into accepting, or at least acknowledging, a version of reality that we would usually ignore or refuse to notice.

I am asking you to grow. I am asking you to accept that you matter. I am asking you to accept that you are important. I am asking you to accept that you are special. I am asking you to set yourself free.

Make a quick mental list right now of your closest friends and family. Got it?

Now, how many of those amazing, special people never accept or appreciate how amazing and special they are even when they are told?

Have you ever considered, even for a second, that you are one of those amazing, special people? I wonder if your friends made the same list right now, how many would put you on it?

It's time for 'normal' to stop. It's time for you to accept, even on a teeny weeny level, that you are better than you think you are. If you can do that then you are breaking the illusion that Laing talks about. You will have noticed what you failed to notice.

Think about what it is you want to change most in your life just now. Now, what is it that you are pretending to ignore or refusing to notice that stops it changing?

Here's an example that might be familiar to you. I was coaching a client recently who was absolutely insistent that, despite her stellar CV, there were simply no jobs for which she was qualified.

She was completely wrong and in fact hadn't even bothered to look because her belief was so strong.

I asked a few simple questions about what kind of position she wanted and a quick web search popped up a whole heap of matching jobs.

That's when an interesting thing happened – in order to keep her belief intact she came up with a qualifying statement to allow herself to ignore the reality of the list of jobs I found. She decided that none of those jobs would match her current salary and she was quite definite on this.

I refined my search to take her salary needs into account . . . and proved her wrong again!

The jobs will all be too far away. Wrong again.

She was getting desperate now. She has no skills that the companies offering these jobs would value. A quick conversation with one of the companies proved this one wrong.

She couldn't keep it up. She couldn't continue failing to notice. And once I helped her notice, she realised it wasn't as scary as she thought it was going to be.

Her negative belief crumbled and she is now in a job she loves.

Right now, how many things that would change your life do you think you are failing to notice? Amazing jobs, relationships, possibilities and opportunities. What if, all it would take to notice them is for you to reject what you think is 'normal' and go looking?

In my experience the world is filled with endless choices. I accept some of them may be more hidden than others, but no-one said that the path to awesomeness would be obvious!

There is *always* choice and if you don't think this applies to you, then I dare you to prove me wrong. Please write to me and let me know about all the choices you don't have. I guarantee I can help you find some! I'm not saying you will like them all but tough choices are still choices.

I find when we take the time to notice what is going on in our lives it becomes infinitely easier to accept that things are better than they seem. With that in mind, take your time over this next exercise.

When I did this the first time it took at least half an hour even though, on the face of it, it looks simple. I have known people to need much more time to get it finished. Take all the time you need and don't stop until it is completed. This one really does need a notebook or sheet of paper.

The seven things exercise

1. Write down seven things you are good at

    Be honest and push through any 'I'm not good at anything' internal chat. Everyone is good at something. Get at least seven before you move on. No cheating!

2. Write down seven things you love to do (whether you currently do them or not)

    I'm not asking how you do it, how often or even if it is financially or logistically possible just now, I am just asking what you LOVE to do. Be open and honest.

3. Write down seven things other people tell you that you are good at

    Don't do yourself the disservice of pretending these things don't exist. Be honest, pay attention and accept the compliment however uncomfortable it makes you feel!

This exercise will create a 'map' of who you really are rather than the limited version you pretend to be. If it were up to me you would now look at this page every morning before you start your day to remind yourself of how special you are.

And notice something for me, how was your internal voice during that exercise? Did it get in the way and try to take away from what you have written? Did it stop you completely by telling you the exercise was pointless or half an hour was way too long? Or was it quiet and supportive?

I wonder, when you think back, if the internal voice was familiar, perhaps so familiar that it was only once I mentioned it that you realised it had even spoken. I wonder how often you fail to notice your own internal chat and what it is saying to you when you aren't paying attention? Is it being a supporter or a saboteur?

So now you know how to stop your mind ignoring important information. Unfortunately that's not the only way your mind is filtering the world around you to keep things 'normal'.

LAST TIME I CAUGHT ONE THIS BIG

At exactly the same time as you are not noticing the real world around you, your bubble is taking the information you do notice and adjusting it to fit your expectations (even if those expectations are bonkers!). I call this 'Twisting'.

Here's a simple example; do you know someone who becomes so stressed and anxious that they begin to experience full blown panic attacks? In certain branches of psychology this thought process is called *'catastrophising'*, i.e. believing the worst might, and more than likely will, happen. Well, the process of anxiety is a perfect example of everything you are learning here.

Let's look at it in a little more detail.

All anxiety is based on the answer to one question, 'What if . . .?'

As soon as this question is asked reality is no longer of any relevance to the imminent emotional explosion. *Everything* that happens from the moment that question is asked is entirely internal and nothing more than perception. We could even go as far as to call it fantasy.

It is important to note here that some people ask the question 'What if . . .?' regularly and never get anxious. These people ask 'What if . . .?' and their mind shows them pictures of success and happiness and amazing things happening and, as we would expect, their mind and body responds as if it was real. Because of the content of their pictures they don't get anxious, they get *excited*.

Remember this the next time something exciting happens in your life. In my experience of speaking to some exceptionally successful people, knowing how to get excited about the future is a key strategy in their success.

I think of anxiety and excitement as being next-door neighbours. The process starts with the same question but the feeling you get completely depends on which door you go through. Positive door = excitement, negative door = anxiety.

That's why, if someone asks the question 'What if . . .?' and their mind shows them a picture of the worst possible scenario, their mind and body will, of course, respond as if it is really happening, even if they know rationally and sensibly that the worst case scenario is ridiculous or even impossible.

What the mind sees, it feels and, since they obviously don't want this negative thing to happen, they feel the protective emotion of anxiety. Their internal world is screaming at them to get to safety and get there quick!

The feeling of anxiety will continue for as long as the worst case scenario movies continue to run inside their mind and this whole process can go from a standing start to a full blown panic attack in a matter of seconds.

However, as we have seen, it is important to remember that *it is not real.*

- It is simply Thought = Feeling = Action.

- It is only 'real' inside your bubble.

- It is only ever as 'real' as the lemon.

- Excitement and anxiety are actually nearly identical. The only difference is the picture inside your head.

And this happens every single day to every single one of us and it happens in a similar way with every single emotion you feel.

Imagine if happiness could work like anxiety and you spent time making yourself blissfully ecstatic every day simply by running pictures of all the amazing things you were going to do and achieve that day.

Why isn't that totally possible for you?

Your world will be how you *expect* it to be and your bubble is distorting the world to make sure it stays that way!

Think about your favourite band. Now, be honest, how many people do you know that think your favourite band are total rubbish?!

In a similar way to our football fans earlier, you both listen to the same band playing the same music, but experience it differently. You have probably even tried to convince them and played them your favourite song only to find even that doesn't work. They still don't like it! And with what we have learned now, it's fairly easy to understand why. It's good music *to you*. Not to them.

Your experience of that music contains special memories, amazing moments, that concert you went to and the time you and that special person stayed up listening to that album until 4am talking about how life would be perfect if everyone did things your way! Other people might like the same music while still experiencing it differently to you and for different reasons. To others it's still just noise!!

Here is one of the simplest ways to prove that your mind perceives the world how it wants to rather than seeing the reality.

This image shows two lines of equal length, you can measure them if you like.

I promise, the following image is *exactly* the same two lines with some simple additions. Now, do they still look equal?

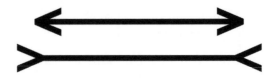

The lines seem to be different lengths because your mind expects them to be. It alters and twists your perception to match what *should* be happening. But it's wrong.

This is the way your world works. You don't perceive what is really going on because your mind perceives your own version, twisted to match your expectations based on all your past experiences. Your mind is doing this to all the information you are exposed to, every single minute of every single day.

Think about how this affects your everyday life.

Every single belief you have is a twisted distortion of reality. Every single one.

And it doesn't matter if you are reading this believing you are the ultimate professional in your field or if you believe you are never going to amount to anything. Whatever you believe, you are likely to find out you are right because your mind will ignore and twist anything that disagrees.

The rest of the world can see the truth but, while you hold a belief strongly in your mind, you will discover that your mind ensures that every piece of evidence backs up what you believe.

I once had a client who I'll call Bob. He had some difficult times as a kid, especially in his teenage years, and most of these difficult times involved his mum. As an adult, his relationship with his mum was his biggest issue and caused problems throughout his life, including having a detrimental effect on his relationships and career.

But here's the thing, all of these issues stemmed from one, seemingly insignificant incident that happened just at the beginning of high school. It was such a fleeting moment that I wouldn't be surprised to discover that his mum didn't even remember it but, for Bob, it was definitely not insignificant. He used it to colour literally everything that happened from that moment on.

Everything he believed himself to be became twisted through this event. This meant that, no matter how much his mum, or anyone else, tried to show love, support, kindness or compassion, Bob couldn't see it. He saw it all as some type of manipulation even when, to everyone else, it was entirely genuine. This one event twisted his relationship with his mum, himself, and many other people, for over 20 years.

Now that I have helped Bob release that hurt from the past, he is living a very nice life where, all of a sudden, no-one is trying to make fun of him! And that's because in reality, they never were.

This, ladies and gentlemen, is your mind working at optimum performance! It creates a mirage of reality around you to convince you that whatever you believe, you are right!!

If you believe you aren't good enough, you will find the evidence to convince yourself you are right.

If you believe you aren't attractive, you will find the evidence to convince yourself you are right.

If you believe you aren't important enough to be loved, you will find the evidence to convince yourself you are right.

If you believe you are lucky (or not), you will find evidence to convince yourself you are right.

From now on, I want you to start noticing when you are making things into what they are not.

I know it's difficult to just stop it happening – the twisting of reality is a natural part of your mind's make up, but it *is* entirely possible to be aware that everything you believe may not actually be true.

What if (there's that question again!) everything you are sensing and thinking only has a *possibility* of being true? What if you were to take time to see the world through a different bubble? How would someone else perceive you? If you didn't believe those things about yourself, how differently would you respond to the world?

We are creatures of routine and pattern and our beliefs are just another pattern. But when we get comfortable or scared we rarely step outside our own 'bubble' to notice what it is that is actually happening in the world.

Remember as we discussed earlier, all of the perceptions you have about the world can be both right and wrong at exactly the same time. Please feel free to read that sentence again, I promise it does make sense!

The question is . . . which perceptions are useful and which ones are not? Let's begin loosening some of your beliefs by seeing the world through a different 'bubble'.

Just one tip before this exercise. You will be climbing 'inside' a bubble other than your own and you should ask yourself if what you are saying is actually what that other person would say and actually how they would say it if you asked them.

How real is your real?

1. Think about a situation that happens regularly in your world that upsets or annoys you.

2. In your own mind, what is going on? What is actually happening when this situation occurs?

3. Now imagine seeing the world through the eyes of another person who is involved in this situation.
   a. How might they be seeing it?
   b. What would they say is happening?
   c. What can you learn from this?

4. And finally, what if you were seeing the world through the eyes of a bystander who knows nothing about what is going on at all?
   a. What would they say about it?
   b. What can you learn from this?

5. Which one of these perceptions is right?*

6. If you were to change your thoughts about this right now, what would be your biggest realisation?

* HINT: if your answer here is 'mine', I'm fairly certain you're wrong!!

Sometimes it just takes a new perspective to change our world. How big was the shift you felt at Step 4?

The thought process of climbing outside your bubble can change relationships in seconds because it challenges the belief that your perception is real. It makes you realise that there are different ways of seeing any one event and allows you to ask yourself what is the most useful way to see a situation. We will return to this concept in chapter 5.

As if ignoring and twisting wasn't enough to convince you that your perception of reality is what you want it to be, your mind has one more trick up its sleeve. It reckons it can predict what is going to happen next.

IT ALWAYS HAPPENS TO ME

You'll know this to be true if you have ever tried to pull a door you should have pushed, pushed a door you should have pulled or even worse, pulled and pushed a door that actually slides! When you walked up to that door your mind makes a prediction based on expectations and patterns, acts accordingly then has the cheek to make you surprised/confused/annoyed if its prediction doesn't come true!

Your mind loves patterns because patterns make life easy and predictable i.e. this happens, then that happens, then this happens and it leads to a predictable result. So it makes *assumptions* based on these patterns.

As a child, the skill of pattern spotting allowed you to apply simple models to a hugely varied world and make sense of it. By learning how 1+1=2, you can also understand that 2+2=4 and that 100+100=200. All of these things use the same idea, the same model and so, by learning one, it makes it so much easier to learn them all.

You learned to walk, talk, make friends, eat, cook, study, type, read, run, literally every single thing in your life, using previous experiences to make educated guesses on how things work, what they do and what they will do next.

Incidentally, this is also where phobias and fears can come from. You have one bad experience with a spider or a dog and all of a sudden you decide that every spider or every dog is a danger. You assume that they are all the same, that they fit the pattern, and so, because you're scared of one, you must be scared of them all.

Do you see how it works? The world you perceive is not the world that is happening in reality. The world you perceive is entirely your version of a world of infinite possibilities. You create your experience of life not the other way round.

Here's another simple example, what model of car did you learn to drive in? And what model of car do you drive now? How did you do that? Did you have to relearn how to drive? Of course not, you have assumed every car works the same way. Even if you happen to drive the same model of car you learned in, it is still likely a different car but that doesn't actually matter or affect your driving ability. All you need to know is the big circle thing steers and the pedals are in the same order as before! As long as you have that, you're off.

Even when challenges are thrown our way and we have to drive abroad or in an automatic, our mind simply adapts the pattern – it doesn't have to start from scratch.

This trait of our minds turns us into a learning machine but it is also the trait that can turn us into creatures of habit and routine. And sometimes habit and routine mean we can become 'stuck'.

How many things do you have a routine for? Do you ever tell anyone you're a 'wee bit OCD' because your routine has reached dizzying levels of organization and repetition? Have you ever asked yourself why? Or are you just too scared to change it in case your life falls apart because the toilet roll isn't on the right way or someone has folded your shirts without the buttons being straight?

We convince ourselves that predictable behaviour means predictable outcomes and this is true at all times, until it's not! The problem with too much routine is the assumption that it will always be that way. But, we all know that's not how the world works. Things are always changing. A creature of habit and routine is easily nudged off course when the world decides that it is going to do something new and, when this happens, many find themselves unable to function. Adaptability is key.

Here's an easy way to test one of your routines to see how much it affects your thinking. Next workday, I want you to try and get ready in a slightly different order. Just do one thing out of its normal place. Brush your teeth before you get dressed or have your breakfast after you get ready. You'll either get confused, a little bit upset or you'll end up sticking with the change in your routine because the new way works better!

And remember how we talked earlier about how we medicate our feelings? Why do we medicate our feelings if it is not out of an *assumption* that if we do this/take this/have this then it will make us feel better?

If our minds were really clever you would think that, after we have that one horrible cigarette on the morning of that awful hangover, our mind should tell us to stop smoking and drinking because it doesn't make us feel nice anymore? But it doesn't. In fact it just assumes that one was bad but the next one will be better! In fact, in time, it will ignore this cigarette, ignore the hangover and you will do it all again.

Why? Because our drug of choice worked well in the past and left a huge positive impression on our mind that we can't forget. Your mind assumes that, because it worked so well that one time way back when, it will work again. The pattern will repeat.

For example, because smoking cigarettes made you feel *über* cool when you were 15 and drinking tequila shots was something you enjoyed when you were 19, somewhere in your bubble you assume that they will work the same way now. However, you're now 32, can't get to the top of the stairs without an oxygen mask and take three days to get over a hangover! Time has moved on but your mind has not!

But let's be honest here, usually our assumptions about our world are largely beneficial. These patterns keep society in order and help all of us learn quickly. They only become a problem when they start hurting or limiting us.

There's an old phrase that bounces around the personal development world that says *'if you always do what you've always done, you'll always get what you've always got'*. And that's exactly what so many of us are doing.

Another of my favourite quotes, and I apologise for not being able to trace the source, says *"if life is so short, why do we do so many things we don't like and like so many things we don't do?"*

This, my friend, is the power of routine and pattern. It's all too easy to end up stuck in a rut, living the pattern, when we assume that getting out of that rut and breaking that pattern will either be difficult or painful.

In fact, because we ignore a whole heap of information that doesn't fit our expectations, many times we are simply failing to notice that our patterns are not permanent. We are actually breaking our patterns all the time however these moments of 'clarity' are often simply overlooked in favour of noticing the routine that we are used to. We tell ourselves that little moment of light is simply a glitch or an accident.

The moment where someone laughs and then tells the world they are sad *all* the time, the moment someone is shown love but minutes later tells the world they have no-one, the moment someone has 10 easy hours without a cigarette because they are flying but then insists they can't survive a two hour drive without stopping for a smoke.

These aren't glitches. These moments are showing you that the world is not as fixed and certain as you think it is. They are potential seeds of change and seeds need energy if they are going to grow. *You* need to be the energy of your own change. *You* need to decide to direct your energy towards the amazing things in your life but all too often we don't because we assume it will be too difficult. It's not difficult, it just needs focus and effort.

When these moments happen, pay attention. Grab them, hold them, and nurture the seeds of change that they provide. Ask yourself how it was that you managed to have that moment of clarity, happiness, calm or confidence. Paying attention to these moments and acknowledging their existence gives that seed the energy to turn into real change.

So that we can start directing your energy towards your seeds of change, lets take a quick trip through your routines. For this next exercise, think about a habit or a routine that you would like to stop. Smoking, drinking, nail biting, road rage are all good examples.

Same stuff, different day

1. Identify something you do or think regularly and wish you could stop.

2. Now thinking back, what has prevented you from changing or stopping this in the past?

3. If you imagine for a second that you no longer do or think that thing, how would you feel now?

4. With that feeling in mind, what action could you take to stop it easily right now?

5. What is the action that you have already taken that would show your mind that you can stop doing this easily right now?

Run this exercise as many times as you like with different routines or habits. I find question 3 is often the one that stumps people but I promise, if you give it thought, you will find the glitches – the places and times where 'normal' doesn't happen.

You live in the world you think you live in. So why not think your world to be awesome?

Re-tuning the mind

Before we move on, let's take a minute to consider a situation in which all the filters of the mind are working at once. We'll use a phobia as an example.

Alison tells the world she is scared of dogs. She is scared because of one, frightening experience when she was very young. Because of that experience she has spent her whole life assuming every dog wants to bite her just like that one did. She has created a generalisation – an *assumption*. This means she has felt the emotions of countless dog bites that have never actually happened, nor are actually going to. She *ignores* the absurdity of this.

Now, here she is, all grown up and when someone introduces her to a wee, cute, fluffy puppy, she freaks out again. Inside her bubble, Alison is not experiencing the cute, fluffy puppy. On the contrary, she has *twisted* the wee fluffy puppy into a big, toothy monster beast and can't work out why no-one else can see it waiting to pounce on her with teeth bared.

No one else can see it because it isn't actually happening.

So now she *twists* people's sympathetic approaches and believes they are laughing at her, which makes her feel silly and self-conscious. Her mind has completely *ignored* the big cute eyes, the fact that the dog is lying on its back getting it's tummy tickled and the fact its teeth are tiny and soft. None of these things matter because of the *assumption* that, in *her* world, all dogs are scary. Therefore her mind *twists* her reality, *ignoring* the truth of the situation, making that fear real and true.

Do you see how it works?

It may not be specifically about dogs for you, but your mind uses the same process every day. The reality you perceive and experience is not the reality that is happening. The reality you perceive is entirely your reality. You are creating it.

What all of this means is that we have all *learned* to be who we are.

The person you believe yourself to be as you sit here reading this book is not who you 'are'. This is just someone you have learned to be. Who you are and how you believe life *should* work is simply the result of all of your experiences up to this moment in your life.

Your mental processes are shaping the world around you to fit your expectations. The only thing stopping you changing the things you want to change is, as Laing said, that you are failing to notice just how many possibilities surround you.

Now ask yourself what would happen if you changed your expectations? What if you could undo that learning? What if it was possible to change who you are, how you feel and what you do? And what if it is all just as simple as cutting pearls off a necklace. . . .?

Chapter 2 in a nutshell:

- It is not your circumstances that affect you; it is your THOUGHTS about those circumstances that affect you.

- Change the thought = change the feeling = change the action = change your life.

- You are ignoring, twisting and making assumptions about your sensory experience every day. *All* of your problems and challenges are based on dodgy evidence.

- Your problems and negative feelings are only as real as the lemon.

- Keep watching for the number 23.

Meeting my match – revisited

We see what we want to see. Our world is what we make it. Our reality is perception and our perception can change in a heartbeat. This was what had frustrated me with Madison – I couldn't seem to break her perception. But then, of course, I asked her that question.

That day is a day I will never forget. Have you ever had the good fortune to be with someone when they get an insight that changes their life and they realise it can all be so much better than they thought it was? It's an amazing and precious thing and that day with Madison was one of those precious moments.

I asked her a question I had never asked her before. I simply asked her,

'What is it that you would have to totally accept
that would allow all of this to change?'

She giggled and asked me not to ask her that! So of course, being ever respectful of the client's wishes, I immediately asked it again. After some more giggling she asked if she could write it down instead of saying it. 'Of course' I replied and she picked up her phone and started typing.

She handed me the phone and it simply said,

'That I am loved'.

Those four words almost instantly transformed her perception of her family, herself and her home life. She had been refusing to believe it to be true but when she typed those words they finally became 'real'. There were goose bumps all round! Her mum and I had a good chat following the session, I explained what had happened and, after a few honest and loving conversations back at home, the air was cleared. If she starts withdrawing, gets angry or starts writing more dark poetry, everyone around her reminds her that whatever she does, she is loved.

And, whether you want to accept it or not, so are you.

Changes in time

On the face of it everyone thought Amy had life sorted. She was in her late 40s, amicably divorced with two grown up kids who were now independent and she was financially pretty comfortable. As a bonus, she didn't look anywhere near her age and her social life would have put many teenagers to shame! Her house was always the weekend party house and, when I would see her, she would tell me stories of the latest post-pub get together back at her place. But despite all of that, the most important thing was always her kids and grandkids; her relationship with her family was a huge focus of pride in her life.

So, with all that going on, where's the problem?

The strange thing was that, some days, Amy just couldn't get herself motivated to do anything. She was in a job she loved and was able to work from home but sometimes, for days at a time, she would lie on the couch and do absolutely nothing at all. When her boss called she would lie about her targets and what she had been doing and then she would have to work ridiculous hours for days to catch up and get everything where it was meant to be. This existence was proving to be incredibly stressful!

She told me her boss had recently changed and that her new boss didn't seem to understand the challenges of working in Scotland when the rest of the team were all based in England. This was, she was sure, the major factor that had caused her lack of motivation.

As we explored her thoughts to find out where these feelings were coming from, I asked the same important question I ask every single client I work with 'where did this feeling begin?'. Every time I asked, Amy became aware that the feeling existed way before her new boss took over. In fact, everything led back to a completely different person. Her mum.

She had memories of following her mum around as a child trying to show her things she'd done at school, looking for a friendly 'well done' or a moment of approval but it never came. She wasn't allowed to go to parties, she was never given praise, she felt controlled and small and stupid.

After this realisation, Amy began to notice that many of the things she had done in her life, and some of the things she was still doing such as those post-pub get togethers, were down to her looking for approval. She just wanted to feel valued and to be told she was doing well. She wanted to be loved.

So now we have found the problem, how are we going to deal with it? Obviously we hopped in a time machine and took a visit to the place where it all started to see if we could 'fix' the past to change the future.

3

The rules that make us

How do you know how to be you?

When you wake in the morning, how is it that you remember to be scared of spiders while at the same time remembering you love strawberry jam on warm toast?

Why is it that nobody ever simply forgets to be 'themselves'?

Have you ever heard of someone arriving in the heat of Tenerife airport and, while waiting patiently to pick up their suitcase, they suddenly remember that they have a flying phobia that they completely forgot to have on the flight?

Of course not. But if you think about it, why is it that we never forget to have a phobia when we find it frighteningly easy to forget so many other things? Why is it that we can go from confident to scared in a heartbeat but so rarely the other way around?

The answer is simple; *The Rules of Life*. Surely you must have noticed them?

Since you were a teeny tiny baby, everyone around you has been teaching you the Rules of Life; your parents, your friends, your teachers, politicians, the media have all been key participants in the development of the rules that you use to navigate the world.

It's these rules that your bubble follows when it ignores, twists and assumes in its efforts to filter your reality and make sense of the world.

It's these rules that tell you how the world *should* be.

Imagine it like this; when you were born you were perfect, a completely pure, blank slate with a capacity to feel a range of emotions but with no rules of when and why you would feel them. Of course you now understand that what we are really saying here is that you lacked the triggers. In fact you were born with only one rule that you will still have to this day;

loud noises and/or falling will cause fear.

Theme park designers and horror movie directors have used this rule for many years but everything else, every single other rule you live by (and every other feeling you feel), you have learned. When you think about it, that means there must have been a time before this version of 'you' existed.

So if you have a fear of flying, there was a time before you had it. You weren't born with it, which means it must have a beginning, a start point.

There was a time when you did believe, with all your heart, that you *were* good enough. There was a time when you didn't over-analyse every little thing that happens, there was a time when your best friend was just someone you knew, there was a time before you knew how to tie your shoes, there was a time when you didn't know any of the things you know now. There was a time before everything.

And it's because there was this time before everything that I can say with total confidence that you were born with the potential to be incredible.

It is important for you to know that you still have all that potential to be incredible inside of you right here, right now, as you read this.

I hope you are fulfilling that potential and, if you are, how did you achieve that? What made you so successful? What made you decide to be fully motivated and never give up? If you're not fulfilling your full potential, what stops you? What stops you being incredible? What stops you being as happy as you can be? What stops you having the life you want rather than the life you have ended up with? What stops you just being able to be the person you know you are inside and show the world the 'real you'? I'll tell you – the rules.

All your successes and all of your perceived failures are down to this unique and personal set of rules that you have been installing and following from pretty much the minute you were born and possibly even before that.

PEARLS OF WISDOM

The easiest way to understand how you become you is to think about a long string of pearls.

Imagine, each pearl represents an individual memory and every single experience you have adds another pearl, or memory in a never-ending, ever-growing string of pearls.

The more feeling packed in to an individual memory (M), the bigger the pearl. So while some may be the size of a grain of sand, others might be vast pearly balloons packed full of emotion and feeling.

This string of pearls is like the DNA for your personality; it is the blueprint for your identity and it's why you never forget to be you.

Since before you were even born, your mind has been constantly recording every single experience you have and laying down these memory 'pearls' that will *never* be forgotten. (I think if we were to market 'The Mind' as a product, the claim, *'contains new improved Magic Memory Pearls™'* would be an exceptionally unique selling point!)

From an incredibly young age (some say as young as just 12–15 weeks after conception), your Magic Memory Pearls™ have been collecting on your string, gathering themselves into bundles of experiences and storing themselves neatly so they can be recalled at a moments notice to guide you through the world.

Let's be honest though, a good proportion of the pearls that end up on your string will never be recalled again. These are the 'grain of sand' memories. It's very unlikely that a trip to the local supermarket to buy milk one grey, dreary Wednesday in November will alter your life in any significant way. On their own, such everyday memories just don't carry the emotional 'weight' or meaning required to change the direction of your life.

Instead they are simply stored somewhere deep inside your mind and, as they collect together, they contribute to the patterns and assumptions we talked about before. For example, how do you know where the milk is in your local shop? Ever had the experience of going to a particular aisle for a particular something only to find it's not where it's 'meant' to be?

These 'grains of sand' build our expectations and our basic rules.

For now we are more concerned with the rules that change our lives and those are only formed when we become emotionally involved. Imagine that, on our string of pearls, emotion and meaning equals weight – the more weight a rule holds, the more important it will be to us.

There are two ways that MMPs can put enough weight into your string to change the way you think, feel and behave forever. There is the life-altering whack of a Big Bang and the more subtle, destiny bending nudge of a Drip Feed.

BIG BANGS

Imagine you have popped into your local supermarket (again!) and, as you stand contemplating which biscuits you are going to buy and then feel bad about eating later on, you spark up a conversation with an attractive and interesting stranger. Experience (aka your MMPs) immediately tells you that they are just your 'type'.

This new person fascinates you, intrigues you, sparks you and leaves you with an amazing buzzy, excited tingle inside.

When you get home you try your best to concentrate on other things but all night you can't stop thinking about this person you met and that tingly feeling you had.

Even the next day at work you are on a high. In fact, you feel great for days, running the brief conversation over and over again, imagining conversations that haven't yet happened. You think about what would happen if you met again, deciding exactly what you would say if you were to meet them in the supermarket again.

This excites you so much, you even start going back to the super-market at the same time, every single day in the hope you will bump into them again. Every time you walk through the door, you get excited, "What if . . .?" you ask yourself. "What if something special was to happen this time?"

What if indeed . . .

This is just one example of a Big Bang. One hugely emotional experience and the aftershock of that experience changes how you think, feel and behave for a long period of time, potentially forever.

To put it simply, there's a big emotional **BANG!** and everything changes. And I mean everything. A Big Bang can fundamentally change you as a person. Our tale of supermarket romance is relatively simple but think about how your life has been affected by exam results, the death of someone close, accidents, births, bad flights, scary childhood moments, sudden changes or actually any moment in time that, even as you sit here right now, you can still remember exactly how it felt.

The importance of meaning

These individual and highly emotional moments of time will change how you think about the world. As you know, any new way of thinking will give you a new way of feeling because,

Thought = Feeling = Action

Your bubble has been re-tuned, and you will now experience the world in a new and different way.

So, one sunny Thursday in July, you look over by the apples and your special person is back in the supermarket. You catch their eye, you both smile and you feel a rush of excitement closely followed by an emotional soup of other emotions including fear, happiness and a feeling you remember having once in high school but can't actually name!

All of this happens in a heartbeat. But why? And how is it possible? You only met them once. How does your mind know to give you all these things?

Well, let's slow it all down and take a look at the process behind emotions

When we say,

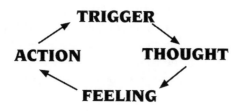

The 'Thought' is actually a simple question,

> *'What does this thing that is happening right now mean to me?'*

Your mind does this with everything – people, work, family, food, cars, love, money, life, the whole lot of it. This is the process you use to access your deepest rules because every time you ask that question, the only way your mind can know the answer is to bring back every Magic Memory Pearl on your string that relates to the experience you are having right now.

In our current example, the Big Bang is that original meeting in the supermarket but remember that any big emotional experience can become a Big Bang, both negative and positive ones. A horribly bumpy night flight through a thunder storm, passing your driving test, asking out your biggest childhood crush, the day you graduated, when you lost someone special, the moment you realised you were in love, when you landed your dream job.

Your mind works the same way for all of these, it uses them to 're-tune' your bubble because of what that moment *means*. Because these events mean so much to you, even though they are only a small moment in time, they will literally change your destiny.

If you drive, think how much that moment you passed your driving test changed your life. It wasn't just about the pass. It was about all the freedom you suddenly had, all the places you could go, even how much more popular you were going to be with your pals. It was about what passing meant to you as a person and it was massive. Yet now, in the context of your life since then, I would guess that your driving test probably counts as one of the smaller Big Bang moments.

Here are three questions on your Big Bangs. Whether you are running through them in your head or writing them down, take a quiet moment to yourself and really work on recalling them. It will be worth it.

Moments of destiny

1. What do you think are the three most significant, emotional events to have happened to you in your life, good or bad?

2. How did they change you?

3. What is the most positive change you have made in yourself because of each of these events?

There is a reason for asking these questions. When you take the time to notice, you find that every Big Bang good or bad, is a lesson. If you answered number 3 with 'there has been no positive change', I challenge you to go back and think more. I'm not suggesting it wasn't difficult and I fully accept whatever happened was hugely emotional, but I promise you that you will have changed something because of that moment and you will have changed it for the better.

Keep thinking. . . .

DRIP FEEDS

Remember we left our potential supermarket romance on a sunny Thursday in July with a second meeting of eyes and a smile? Put yourself back in the story.

You are caught in a heartbeat. Your mind looks inside to decide what your current situation means and, in a split second, it is summing up a lifetime of memories into a feeling that you can understand. You race back along your string of pearls, gathering *every* memory where you have ever spoken to someone you don't know, *every* memory where you have spoken to someone you think is attractive, *every* memory where you have acted on impulse, *every* memory where you have done anything remotely like this before. And then you add them all up.

The sum of all these memories will decide your next action.

The majority of these memories are small moments in time that are relatively difficult to individually recall; a day in school when you caught eyes with someone across a classroom, a passing comment from a relative lost in the depths of time, many days of your childhood watching your parents do what they do. None of these individual memories even come close to the emotional intensity of a Big Bang but when you add them all together, they have combined 'weight'.

This is a Drip Feed, a collection of less emotional memories, stretched out over time, that carry the same meaning.

You will have this experience with friendships, money, career, family, your relationship with food, drink, shopping, exercise, and a whole heap more.

If you drive, think about all you have learned since you passed your test and realise just how much more confident you are as a driver now than you were then. Even if you still don't feel the most confident of drivers, I guarantee that you are more so now than you were when you first passed your test. So let me ask, when specifically did you learn to be a more confident driver? When did you gain the knowledge to be able to drive away from a set of lights while simultaneously peeling a banana?[1]

Was there a special course? Was there a particular day when you thought 'Yep, that's me now. I'm a confident driver who can peel bananas and push pedals at the same time?'[1] For most of us the answer will be no. In fact, it will be near impossible to pinpoint. It apparently just happened.

This is how a Drip Feed works. You don't notice it happening, you don't notice things changing. It just happens and you just change.

Imagine we meet 18 year old identical twins. One works as an artist while the other goes off to join the Army. As they embark on their new careers they have a set of very similar values and personality traits because the majority of their Drip Feeds and Big Bangs to this point have been shared and their rules are therefore very similar.

Now, let's meet them again after four years in their very different careers.

To keep it short, one of the twins has been regimented, trained and moulded by the discipline of the Army while the other has spent the years travelling freely around the world, painting as and when they feel like it and indulging their expression and passion for the

---

[1] Disclaimer: neither the author nor the publishers in any way endorse the peeling of bananas while driving. It's a metaphor!

arts. Now, they might still look the same (and some deeper quirks of shared behaviour will have survived), but would you really think it likely that they would still share the same values and outlook on life and the world?

I don't think so either!

A Drip Feed is very subtle and yet it is also our most common way of learning. In fact, almost all of your deepest and most fundamental personality traits will have been learned this way. When did you learn how to love, trust, make friends? It just happened, didn't it?

Or did it? Have a go at these questions and let's see if we can smoke out some of your Drip Feed moments.

The creation of you

1. Complete these three sentences with the first thought that pops into your mind.
   a. I am . . .
   b. I am not . . .
   c. I like to . . .

2. When were you taught each of these?

3. What is your earliest memory of them being that way and can you remember a time even before that?

4. Who were your most important teachers for each of these?

5. How would your life be different if you hadn't learned them?

Realising that you are significantly more in control of your own learning and development than you thought is an important step in becoming who you want to be. Any time you tell yourself 'that's just who I am' I want you to remember that simply isn't true. Whatever and whoever you are is whatever and whoever you have learned to be and that does not have to be fixed. There is always more to learn.

How does the supermarket story end? Well, I'll leave it up to you. . . . Now that you are aware of and understand that you have your own set of rules, consider that whatever ending you choose for our story will likely give you an insight into many of them!

MAGIC MIRRORS

So let's get back to that question your mind unconsciously asks a million times every day;

'What does *<insert trigger here>* mean?'

This question shapes destinies, drives every emotion you feel, creates love, fear, empathy, hate, war, peace and is so fiendishly simple that if we just understood it earlier it may save us great big bucketfuls of struggle and confusion. We can even simplify it a bit more.

Your mind's most important question is really just . . .

'. . . and that means?'

Three of the most powerful words we will ever ask. You are even asking it unconsciously right now.

Whatever you are doing, wherever you are, somewhere in your mind is taking in all the information around you right now, everything you can see, everything you can hear, everything you are feeling and, just for completeness, everything you can smell, and asking '. . . and that means . . .?'

For example, if you are reading this book on a plane and the plane hits a pocket of turbulence, your mind will pose itself the question '. . . and that means . . .?' Now, even though the majority of your mind is focusing on reading the book, a part of your mind will be looking for the rule about turbulence. In a split second, it assesses the 'weight' of all your previous flying experiences, sums them up into an average 'meaning' and then decides how you will feel and behave in response.

The plane has started bumping up and down **and that means . . .?**

a. that the plane is going to fall from the sky like a stone.

b. nothing at all, turbulence is just changes in air pressure, like waves on the sea. Everything is OK.

c. that the wings are going to fall off and then the plane is going to fall from the sky like a stone.

d. I have woken from my nice relaxing sleep and now I'll read for a bit. Are we nearly there yet?[2]

This experience will be familiar to anyone with a fear of flying. Every noise, shake, change in cabin pressure is over-analysed and often given a really scary meaning. And by this point in the book

---

[2] The correct answer to this question is 'b' however we will also give full marks for 'd'!

I hope you are beginning to realise that the experiences that create that meaning do not even need to be real. It is entirely possible, and more common than you might think, for someone to be scared of flying when they have never physically set foot on a plane!

Hearing other people tell scary stories of their plane experiences, seeing frightening plane related material on the news or in a film, or just plain [pun intended!] making it up, it doesn't matter. Just like the lemon in chapter 2, every thought, real and imagined, will be experienced as if it was real. Give yourself enough of them, and you can properly freak yourself out about something you've never even done!

For example, if you are scared of bungee jumping, I might ask if you have ever done a bungee jump? And if your answer is 'no', how do you know to be scared?

This is a vital understanding and it is really, really important to your future.

If you accept that it is possible for someone to install a *fear* of flying without setting foot on a plane then logically it would follow that it is also possible for someone to install a complete *acceptance* of flying without ever setting foot on a plane. Does that make sense? It must go both ways. If you can install fear then you must be able to install confidence in exactly the same way.

Change does not go one way; if you can change negatively then you must also be able to change positively. You just have to want to change.

And now it gets exciting, because if it is possible to change how you respond to flying without even ever being on a plane then it must be possible to change how you respond to love, money, spiders, food, exercise, job interviews, exams and in fact any trigger event that people tend to believe is scary.

Just allow that thought to sit with you for a few moments.

Asking '. . . *and that means* . . .?' is exactly how you know how to behave in a relationship, in your job, with your friends. This is how you know what music you like and what clothes suit you, this is how you know what you like to eat and where you would like to go on holiday. This is how you know if you like to be at big parties or sitting at home in your onesie.

This is how you know how to be you.

You can apply the above example in any of your major life contexts,

---

My relationship is now bumping up and down (and not in a good way) **and that means . . .?**

a. that my relationship is going to fall from the sky like a stone.

b. nothing at all, these bumps are totally normal. Everything is OK.

c. that the wheels are going to fall off and my relationship is going to fall from the sky like a stone.

d. I have woken from my sleep and now I feel much better. I'm sorry. Let's make up.[3]

---

[3] I don't know the right answer to this one. Sorry! Trust yourself, you know what to do.

Every single decision you make is based on a lifetime of learning.

Your MMPs decide what something means and what something means will define your rules about life and, therefore, your MMPs make you 'you'.

You have been, and continue to be, moulded by your experiences and, once you accept this is true, you will keep coming back to the same conclusion; you are not who you think you are.

You are who you have learned to be.

You can be anyone. It just so happens you are 'you', at least for now.

This person you think you are as you read this book is just a version of 'you' moulded from a particular set of random occurrences, coincidences and circumstances. Now, let's hope those occurrences, coincidences and circumstances have made your whole life awesome and amazing in every way. However, if for some reason you don't think life is awesome and amazing in every way, or if you are carrying around an issue, phobia, fear, sadness, anger or anything else that stops you being the special person I know you are, then there are only two reasons for that,

• You have some really big and really heavy Big Bangs and Drip Feeds that you need to let go of.

or

• You have simply failed to notice that you have actually been awesome and amazing for ages!

You are not your thoughts. Thoughts are something you have – they can, and do, change all the time. You are far more than you think you are.

OK, so now you know what has been standing in the way of your awesomeness, how do you get it out of the way?

Well, although your perception of your past may fade with time, your memories are actually stored forever in your subconscious mind. The emotions you attach to those memories are based purely on *meaning*, so what would happen if the meaning of a particular memory changed?

What if, by changing how you feel about things you have experienced in the past, you can change how you feel about the things you are experiencing in the present?

If you ask yourself "what does that memory mean?" and then you take the time to work out why your mind keeps showing it to you, as we will discuss further in the next chapter, you will discover that it is not trying to upset you, it is trying to teach you.

All you have to do is pay attention and allow yourself to become aware of the lesson it is teaching.

Think about a memory of an event in your childhood that really upset you for a long time after it happened, but when you think about it now feels a bit silly, childlike or trivial.

Now, looking back over your string of pearls, when did that memory lose its emotional weight? And why was that?

I guarantee it lost its emotional weight because you realised or learned something about yourself or that memory that you hadn't noticed before.

For instance, when you realise and actively accept that you are a good person, that you deserve to be loved, that it absolutely wasn't your fault and/or that everything is, was, and will be OK, then your mind *will* change that memory accordingly.

You might have let thoughts like these pass through your mind before but allowed the meaning to be lost under the weight of a lifetime of MMPs telling you it's not true. Well, the good news is that you can take that lesson and apply what you have learned to where it is needed most, the specific point of time at which it all began.

Here's an exercise that you can do quickly and easily. It asks some simple questions which have deeply significant answers. If you could send a message back through time to a critical point in your life where a big change happened in your world, what would that message say? What do you know now that you wish the younger you could have known then?

The answers 'nothing' or 'I don't know' are banned!

This exercise can be done quite easily in your head but can be given extra power and significance if you take the time to write it out.

My game, my rules

1. If you could pinpoint a Big Bang, or the beginning of a chain of Drip Feed events that changed your life in a significant way, what would it be? Trust your instinct on this.

2. Imagine you had a time machine right now that can whisk you back to just as that was all starting, what knowledge or insight do you have now that you would teach that younger version of you?

3. Flipping it round, if you had the benefit of that insight or knowledge back then, how would it have changed the event?

4. Who would you forgive or say sorry to?

5. And if you had learned that lesson at that time, how would it have changed how you responded to all the things that came after it?

6. How will understanding this change you now?

If you have written this out, you now have the option of writing a letter to your younger self and explaining exactly all the things you failed to notice back then. Did you realise that there were things you couldn't possibly control? Did you realise you had to let those things go? Did you realise that you were a good person and none of it was your fault?

FORGIVENESS

Before we move on, a brief note on forgiveness. Forgiveness is one of the most powerful aspects of this exercise and is a skill you should practise every day. It's too easy to hold a grudge and say 'I can never forgive' but let me ask you . . . who is hurt by that? Is it the person to whom you are sending your dark thoughts? Or is it you?

Does the person against whom you hold the grudge even know that you hold that grudge? That person you knew 25 years ago and, to this day, you still can't say their name without grimacing. Do they feel bad every time you do that? Or is it just you that feels bad?

It's you. Every single time. This is the emotional equivalent of trying to physically hurt someone by continually punching yourself in the face while screaming, 'Ha, that'll teach you'!!

Forgiveness is never about the other person; it's about you. Forgiveness is not about accepting that whatever happened was right, good or in any way acceptable. Forgiveness is about saying that you are done with it. That it is now time to put that event, that person, in your past and leave them there. If you decide to stop hurting yourself by thinking about it, you can simply accept that they had a reason to do what they did and that reason had nothing to do with you. Forgiveness isn't about rolling over or being weak, in fact it is the ultimate expression of strength. It is the moment you reclaim your life as your own and permanently shut the door on demons from your past.

I know you may think I'm making this sound too easy but you can do this right now. You can let go of a lifetime of pain by simply imagining the past and saying 'I forgive you'.

If you can let the lesson in and forgive the past, it will change your memories of that time and it will change your reality.

BREAKING THE ILLUSION

For someone who is experiencing fear, anxiety, depression, addiction, anger, jealousy, heartbreak or any of the other myriad negative emotions that we have the capacity to feel, it is a difficult concept to grasp that *any* of these feelings could possibly be there to teach us lessons about how to be happier and have more of what we want.

As you have just learned, that is exactly why they are there.

Every single emotion that you feel is a guide and a teacher.

But is it really possible for someone feeling the helplessness of depression to understand that these feelings have the positive intention of making them happier in the long run? How can someone, paralysed by social anxiety and too terrified to connect with another person, understand that the feelings are there to move them towards a place of calm and fulfillment?

I, Brian Costello, hereby promise that every feeling you ever feel, every thought you ever have and every action you ever take is there to help you. Each and every one, dark and light, is there to make you happier, calmer, content, fulfilled and give you more of what you want. Every. Single. One.

The reason you can't see this is because you are simply too close to the feelings. It's too easy to become so wrapped up in how you feel that you can't see what's right there in front of you. In fact, you may even find yourself talking about the positive reason behind your feelings and not even appreciate what you have just said!

You are just not able to see the bigger picture.

It's easier to see it in action when we realise how we do it to others.

Imagine a parent is frustrated at their child because they are not studying for their exams. The parent is anxious because their kid appears to be making the same mistakes they did when they were at school and they remember all the pain those mistakes caused them. They just want their kid to achieve all their potential and have an easier life than they did at that age saying, 'I know if they put the work in now they won't have to put up with all the crap I did when I was a teenager'. Because of all their memories of the past and their desire to see their child succeed, they begin to become frustrated at what they see as a lack of attention or care and that frustration begins to leak out as anger. And the excuse is that 'I'M ONLY SHOUTING BECAUSE I WANT YOU TO DO WELL'.

Remember, we know the intention hidden behind the shouting is to help their child do their absolute best and achieve their potential. But that's not what their son or daughter experiences. No, they experience a parent who won't stop shouting, apparently filled with incredible anger and frustration. And all they really want and need is a little bit of reassurance, support and love.

It's difficult for both parent and child to realise that somewhere, hidden behind the really loud voice, is all the love and understanding support they need.

Here's a phrase to remember;

we judge others by their actions
and
ourselves by our intentions

It is intensely liberating when you witness negative actions in a person and are able to understand the positive intention behind their behaviour. You find that any anger and frustration you might feel in response almost instantly melts away. You realise that, although you may have been the recipient of their behaviour, it isn't actually about you and that their anger isn't actually anger at you, but rather at something inside them.

It is even more liberating when you learn to do this to yourself. This is one way to break the illusion that your pearls from the past control your present and future. This is how you begin to change who you are, and become who you want to be.

In the example above the parent's intention is obviously to help, to show love and support and help someone they love and care for become the best they can be. But it is also obvious that, from another perspective, that is a million miles away from the message that is actually being received.

And, as you start to think about it, how true is this of your own mind?

How often do you judge your own emotions by only thinking about how they make you feel? Do you ever ask the question 'why am I feeling this feeling?'. I bet if you do ask that question, you often look for an external reason to explain things. For example, 'it's because he/she made me feel this way', 'it's because life is unfair', 'it's because I'm not good enough to do what I want to do'. This is normal, we all do it. But now you know there's another way.

When you next ask 'why?' take a moment to actively look for the positive intention behind the feeling and then ask what you can learn from that.

There is a very famous poem by Rumi called The Guest House that sums it up beautifully,

The dark thought
The shame
The malice.
Meet them at the door laughing and invite them in.
Be grateful,
For whatever comes
Because each has been sent as
A guide from beyond

We are often too caught up in blame, anger, frustration, despair and negativity to realise that *every* emotion is a mirror on our internal world.

When we become angry it is often because one of our internal rules has been broken and we feel helpless or scared. We become angry and tell someone how deeply we feel about it to stop it happening again.

When we feel fear or anxiety it is often because we are feeling unsafe or threatened by something external to us. We want to run away but only to keep ourselves safe and protected.

When we feel sad, it is most often due to a sense of loss. We just want back whoever or whatever we have lost.

When we feel guilt or shame, it is often because we have broken one of our own rules, whether intentionally or unintentionally. Guilt motivates us not to break that rule again.

All of these scenarios will be familiar to you and now you know how to change the way you respond. You have learned that each of your emotions, feelings and thoughts is a teacher or, as Rumi suggests, a guide.

TAKING IT TO THE EDGE

To round off this chapter, let me simplify everything just a little more. In moments when our rules drop away and we are left thoughtless, we return to our emotional equilibrium – a special place of balance and stillness. We have a name for this place. We call it Happiness.

Happiness is effortless.

Being unhappy takes lots of work.

If you don't agree, then let me ask you this . . . how much work do you put into being unhappy? Or to put it another way, how much time and energy do you put into preventing yourself from being happy?

- by being frustrated at other people's actions?

- by not backing down and saying sorry?

- by being anxious about circumstances you can't control?

- by making sure you never forget those horrible 'Big Bang' moments of your past, running them in your head every day and telling yourself you will never forget them?

What would happen if you stopped doing all this right now? I bet the answer to that is the same in all cases.

You'd be happier.

But that's easier said than done isn't it?

We don't back down because we want to be right, we don't chill out because we don't want to be hurt, we become anxious because we want to find safety away from anything that scares us so we can be calm.

Notice that everything we want is positive – to be loved, to be safe, to be calm – but the methods we use to try to achieve them often cause us pain.

Your mind is a logic machine and is far more ordered than you think. It is almost simplistic and childlike in its logic because a large proportion of the rules that we use to make our decisions were laid down in childhood.

Scared? Run away.

Hurt? Avoid the cause of the pain.

Helpless? Feel sad.

When you break it down, it really is the most simple elegant logic. And, as you now know, all decided by your rules.

As I said before, you were born perfect, a completely pure, blank slate with a capacity to feel a range of emotions but with no rules of when and why you would feel them. You weren't born angry, you weren't born frustrated, you definitely weren't born with the ability to look back over the past and only concentrate on bad stuff. These behaviours are learned according to your rules, your rules are defined by experience and your experience is simply adding pearls to a string.

Chapter 3 in a nutshell:

- Your life is governed by a set of learned rules that affect every thing you do.

- You can spot the existence of your rules by noticing the meaning you attribute to events, people and other triggers.

- Your rules have been taught through a series of significant emotional memories which can be divided into two types, Big Bangs and Drip Feeds.

- Big Bangs tend to be individual, emotional, short term experiences that instantly change our behaviours.

- Drip Feeds are long chains of experiences that change our behaviour over time.

- The meaning of your memories can and do change. It is your choice whether you do that changing on purpose or not.

- We tend to judge ourselves by our intentions and others by their actions.

- There are no accidental thoughts and every single thought you have is there to help you in some way.

Changes in time – revisited

Have you ever heard of a Prince Rupert's Drop? When molten glass is dripped into cold water a tear drop shaped glass 'bead' is formed which has some interesting properties, being that it is both exceptionally strong and exceptionally weak at the same time.

It is so strong, you can take a hammer to the 'bulb' end and it will simply bounce off. At the other end, if you simply snap a small piece off the 'tail', the whole drop will immediately and explosively turn to dust! (have a look online for some amazing slow-mo videos of this phenomenon).

Well, every one of your problems is just like these Prince Rupert's Drops. They may appear to be fixed and strong when you look at them as they happen in the present, but back at the beginning, where they were first formed, they are fragile, weak and easy to break.

I helped Amy access a really clear memory from about 6 years old. She had sneaked out of the house to go to a friend's birthday party after being told she couldn't go. Her memory was of being in the back seat of a car that her mum was driving home after she had been dragged from that birthday party in front of all of her friends. She remembered her mum turning from the front of the car and snarling 'You wait until you get home'. That little 6 year old girl felt incredible fear and a life time of seeking approval began.

But now, as we revisited it, that fear lived in the past and we could change it. I asked her if she could go back and speak to that 6 year old 'her' now, what she would teach her. Her answer?

"You are a bigger person than she is".

She cried as she said this and, in that instant, that 6 year old stopped being scared. She imagined sitting in the back of that car feeling resilient, strong, and capable. She realised her mum couldn't hurt her any more and she no longer needed anyone's approval. And, just like the drop, as soon as she snapped that little bit off the tail, the rest of that chain of memories immediately and explosively turned to dust. She forgave her mum, she realised that she never meant to cause pain. She was doing the best she could at the time and Amy suddenly realised that it was because of this that *she* was now such a positive, attentive and loving mum to her own kids. In a funny way, she was grateful.

She changed so much after that session. She stood up to her boss and got her job back to where she wanted it to be. She stopped lying on the couch for days on end and her house stopped being 'party central' as she realised that she was only inviting everyone back there because she was worried they wouldn't like her if she said 'no'. She rediscovered her motivation and appreciation for work, life and herself and all it took was a quick trip back in time to where it all began.

Where did it all change for you?

Doing the right thing

Declan came to see me because he was having some trouble finding direction in his career. He had recently been made redundant and had some very important choices to make about what he was going to do next. He knew that his confidence was low as the final couple of years of his job had been far from happy and being made redundant had actually come as a relief. However, his wife was very pregnant, they had a two year old already and that meant he needed a new job quickly. Declan had no idea what he wanted to do now, only that it had to be nothing like what he had been doing before.

By the time Declan and I actually got together for our first session, I was pleased to learn that he had already found a new job. In his own words, it wasn't perfect but was on the right lines with opportunities for promotion and progression. But to Declan none of that really mattered since, even at this early stage, he was apparently doing an amazing job at completely messing it up!

His problem? Well, as he explained it to me, he discovered very quickly after starting that his confidence wasn't actually low after all, it was completely non-existent! He was nervous, made silly mistakes and frequently found himself unable to make even the simplest of decisions.

Despite his growing experience in the role, his new colleagues were beginning to notice his mistakes and they were becoming no less frequent. This was not the type of supportive workplace environment where someone was likely to come over, put a friendly arm round his shoulder and ask if everything was OK. This was the type of place where he would be out the door as quickly as he came in if he didn't start performing!

He had become very anxious about this and with good reason. The new baby had arrived, his wife was now on maternity leave and all he could think about was how everything was going wrong. No matter what he tried he couldn't break the cycle.

He told me he felt broken. Interestingly he also said he felt that his mind had become his enemy.

I explained to him that though it may feel that way sometimes, your mind is never really your enemy. As you now know, nothing your mind does is an accident, everything has a purpose.

In Declan's case we just needed to find out what the purpose actually was.

4

Cracking your code

Have you ever woken up on a work day and found that the mere thought of being back in the office again just makes you want to curl up in a wee ball under the duvet and pretend it's not happening?

Or, how many times have you decided that right now, this minute is the perfect time to start your diet and exercise regime but then that minute passes quite quickly, the motivation dips and you never make it past the 'thinking about it' stage?

Or, have you ever had a relationship that 'should work on paper' but for some reason is a complete disaster in real life?

Have you ever wondered why?

Maybe life is simply down to luck? Maybe the mind is like a fruit machine. You just pull the handle and hope you get what you are looking for. Keep pulling the handle long enough and eventually you'll win . . . if you're lucky.

Is life just down to chance?

Remember I said earlier that

Thought = Feeling = Action

Well let's get science-y for a second and solve this equation by working it backwards.

If the Action we want is *Change*,

Thought = Feeling = CHANGE

then what is the *Feeling* that logically needs to go before it? Well, we call the energy we use to change the things we want *Motivation*, so let's plug that into the equation,

Thought = MOTIVATION = CHANGE

And what is the thought we use to find *Motivation*? Well, I challenge you to find that thought right now. Go for it. Find a thought that motivates you to do something and run it in your head. It's not a trick, just think of a thought that makes you feel motivated to do something.

Got it? OK good. What did motivation actually *feel* like?

I'm going to take a wild guess here and bet it didn't feel like motivation. It might have felt like excitement, pride, happiness, success, love, connection or a myriad other emotions but it didn't *feel* like motivation.

It didn't *feel* like motivation because the *feeling* of motivation doesn't actually exist.

Am I really telling you that the one thing you need to get the life you want doesn't actually exist? Well, no, I'm not and to say it doesn't exist is perhaps a bit extreme. Look at the image on the next page for a perfect example of what I'm talking about. And look carefully – there is going to be a test!

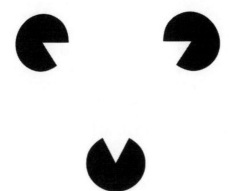

Ready for the test question?

Is there a white triangle in the picture above?

If your answer is 'Yes', you are totally wrong.

This illusion is called The Kanizsa Triangle and I promise you there is no triangle in it. What *is* in the picture are three little pac-man like shapes in the corners where a triangle would be. The triangle itself is an illusion.

And that's a little like motivation. We spend our lives searching and hoping for the feeling of motivation but it's not a feeling in it's own right. Motivation is the result of lots of other feelings coming together.

Confused? Ok, let me clear the whole thing up.

EMOTIONAL SUMS

Why are you currently reading this book?

What is it specifically that has you reading this book, at this stage of your life, on this day, in this place, right now? What is it that motivates you to read it? Because you want knowledge? Because you want to make a change in your life? Because you hope it might give you ways to become happier, more content, more peaceful, calmer? Or is it something else entirely?

Whatever your reason, it isn't motivation. You didn't feel a burst of motivation to pick this book up. And I can say that with confidence because, when you really think about it, the reason you are reading this book is because some other feeling happened and it was *that* feeling that gave you the motivation.

I think it's safe to say that in most cases, you are reading this book in the hope it will make you happier, or give you valuable information, or help you understand and help someone you know and care about. It was those feelings that made you pick the book up.

I would suggest that, in our equation,

Thought = Feeling = Action

it would actually be far more accurate to say that motivation is the *Action*.

Thought = Feeling = MOTIVATION

And this is why we find it so hard to change.

How many times have you waited to *feel* motivated rather than *doing* something that would get you motivated?

In my experience, the more we think motivation is a feeling; the more we become passive in our motivation. Are you not tired of sitting back and wondering why your life doesn't change, why you don't lose weight, why you don't change jobs, why you don't fix or change your relationships, why you're not doing all the things you want to do? We wonder why our lives stay stuck and it is simply because many of us are waiting for a feeling that doesn't exist.

I want you to start being active in your motivation. That starts by realising that life can be how you want it to be but to get all the good stuff, you need to get off your arse and start *making it happen*!

When you think about what you want (and how good it would be if you got it) then your mind will realise there is more out there to have, more out there to feel, more out there to experience and that's what will give you the motivation to change.

Be honest with yourself, how often do you really dream about something you want without following it up with a bunch of negative self-talk about all the reasons it's not going to happen or why you can't have it?

Think about the times when you've been motivated to go get something and then totally sabotaged yourself from getting it. Did the process go something like this?

1. Think of lots of reasons why you want the thing.
2. Feel really hopeful about getting the thing.
3. One thing goes wrong that wasn't in your plan.
4. Start thinking of all the ways it can go wrong.
5. Give up.

**Success happens to people who never stop dreaming.
Failure only exists in the moment you give up.**

The most important thing to do to make the most of the following exercise is to keep going and not stop writing for at least three minutes – set a timer on your phone if that would help – and it's not as easy as it sounds. If your self-talk is not supportive and starts screaming about how silly this exercise is or that you can't get any of these things then remember, it is only trying to keep you safe. Thank it politely and then keep going. This is just part one, we will be back to this later and that means this one works best in your notebook or on a sheet of paper.

Distant dreamer (part one)

Write down a list of everything that you want to have/achieve/feel/do that would mean all your dreams have come true. Do not stop writing for at least three minutes. Think about relationships, health, family, money, material things, career and anything else you can think of. Write everything down even the crazy stuff. You should have things on the list that scare you!!

Now take another three minutes to reflect on the list and listen carefully to what's happening inside your mind.

If you skipped the exercise then just stop for a second and listen carefully to what's happening inside your mind as you justify to yourself all the reasons why you skipped it. How many of those reasons do you say to yourself often? 'I don't have the time', 'I can't be bothered', 'I don't like doing things like that', 'This makes me uncomfortable'. Any of those sound familiar?

And knowing what you now know, ask yourself what your mind is trying to do for you by giving you those reasons. How is it helping? Is it trying to keep you safe? Is it trying to make you better? Does it want to prevent you from being hurt?

For many people it is this internal chatter guiding us to stay safe and comfortable that means we often settle for what we can get rather than what we really want. But all too often, settling for what we can get means settling for second (or even third) best. We don't stretch ourselves, we don't reach for the incredible gifts that life can offer because we think more about how painful it would be to miss out on happiness, success or love rather than how amazing it would be to have them in our lives forever.

For many of us, we don't think we are good enough to have what we want so we never even try.

I'm going to give it to you straight. I feel our relationship has progressed to that stage by now.

It's time for that thinking to stop. It's time to start putting yourself first and, if nothing else, realise that you are just as important as everyone else.

You are important enough to care about.

You are important enough to be loved and for other people to want to be loved by you.

You are important enough to be given every opportunity to shine your light on this world.

You are important enough to have an opinion and for that opinion to be listened to and respected.

Put trust in yourself and give yourself permission to change your life. You are the only one that is preventing it from happening. Ignite inside youself the burning desire for success, love, happiness, excitement, fun, contentment, peace, and anything else you want and think about them every single day.

The charge is set, you just need to light it.

You are important.
You matter.
You deserve happiness.
You deserve to be loved.
You deserve success.

And everything you need, to get everything you want, is inside you right now.

Motivation comes from our feelings. It is not a feeling itself. Motivation comes from the knowledge that whatever it is that you are experiencing, doing, getting, achieving will make you feel something you want to feel. And your mind *loves* that!

I'll prove it. Get your list from part one and let's do part two of the exercise now. Give yourself some time to relax over this one and let yourself get into it. This is not an exercise in thinking; it is an exercise in feeling, so please commit to this and really *feel*.

Distant dreamer (part two)

1. Choose what you think are the three biggest, most achievable dreams from your list.

2. Write down at least five feelings you would get from achieving each of those dreams.

3. Write down at least three positive changes it would make to your life if you made each dream come true.

4. What would you need to know you have inside you to make you take the first steps to achieving each of those dreams today?

Taking the time to concentrate on this exercise can really stir some big emotions to the surface and if, after completing it, you are still not motivated to change you can go back to the beginning and ask yourself what it is that stops you.

It's really similar to the rules we talked about earlier. Since you were born you have been learning that certain feelings feel good. Your mind wants to do anything it can to feel good so, as you move through your life, these feelings become guides for your mind.

So, if you are still struggling with this exercise, ask yourself if it's possible that you have been programmed to feel *safe* rather than challenged or stretched and it is being *safe* that makes you happy.

Only you can know if that's true, but it might help if you understood where these feelings come from.

THE ORIGIN OF 'NORMALITY'

When you were very young, up to the age of about 7, your mind was an open book. You were being guided around your world by the suggestions of others and a lifetime of learning had begun.

At this age, you simply soaked up everything and anything you saw, felt, heard, smelled and tasted to create your very first images and understandings of the world. Your parents, or whoever looked after you, were the single most significant influence on your world (no matter how good or bad they were!)

For the first seven years of your life, your little, nebulous mind learned the most basic of understandings about how the world works.

- The difference between right and wrong.

- The line between good and bad.

- The things that made you happy and sad.

- And, most importantly, the definition of *normal*.

If you can remember when you were this young, you probably remember that your rules were loose and flexible and pretty much anything was possible. You dreamed of being a superhero, a space rocket, a magical princess or a cat. At this age, there were no barriers or boundaries in your world and you believed you could do anything you wanted.

In addition, you had no definition of failure. When something didn't work you tried, tried and tried again even if you were, literally, trying to put a square peg in a round hole or trying to become a cat.

Think about how powerful a concept the absence of failure is.

Imagine if a baby learned to walk using the same mindset we have as adults. They would try once, maybe twice, decide it was too difficult and then just spend the rest of their life shuffling around on their backside!

On the flipside, imagine just what you could be capable of right now if you still learned like you did as a young child with a full acceptance of failure as a completely natural and necessary step on the path to success? How would it be if you decided you wanted to chase one of your dreams and would stop at nothing until it was achieved? If something went wrong, you would simply adjust and go at it again. Just like you did when you learned to walk.

What if your new process for getting what you want from life looked like this . . .

1. Think of lots of reasons why you want the thing.
2. Feel really hopeful about getting the thing.
3. One thing goes wrong that wasn't in your plan.
4. Change your strategy to make sure it doesn't happen again.
5. Succeed!

You would be totally unstoppable!

When you were this young, your internal map of 'normal' hadn't been established and that allowed you to be beautifully, wonderfully free. Free to dream and wish, free to make mistakes and free to never, ever give up no matter how many times you got it wrong.

But, even at that early stage, you were already on an unstoppable, one way track to a version of 'normal' that would define the rest of your life. Even more frustrating is that, at this stage, the concept of what was 'normal' was completely out of your control.

Imagine the different versions of 'normal' these two children will have;

1. One who grows up in the country, is allowed to climb every tree, balance on walls, run as fast as they want and make every day a possible 'broken bone' day.

2. One who grows up in the city, is told to be careful, not to climb too high, to get down off the wall before they fall, to walk in case they trip and make every day a 'risk avoidance' day.

The first child's idea of 'normal' has excitement, adventure and risk, while the other's has safety, security and care. Neither chose their versions of 'normal', they were given to them and so they have both been shaped by their circumstances. Their parents or carers, the surroundings and other aspects of their upbringing moulded them . . . what is 'normal' is defined by their experience.

And exactly the same thing happened to you.

Your 'normal' is different from everyone else's 'normal' because yours was created by the world in which you were brought up. The origins of this are laid down up to the age of 7 when your mind, in its blissful state of openness and awareness, was guided by the world that surrounded you. As you watched how the world worked, you assumed that what you saw, felt, heard and experienced was 'normal' and this became the blueprint for your life.

For example, to a child who is born blind, blind is simply 'normal' and they have never known anything else. To someone that has known sight and has then lost it, the concept of blindness can be emotionally very painful as they have a different idea of the 'normal' world.

Substitute blindness for love and cuddles or rejection and loneliness and you see how easy it is to have your 'normal' worldview shaped by your earliest experiences. Someone whose early experiences teach them to expect love will miss it if it is not there. Someone who learns to expect rejection may find it difficult to accept love as they constantly prepare for it to be withdrawn.

Can you see how this works? It's just like our goldfish in chapter 2.

So what were your earliest versions of 'normal'? Your life may be very different now but think back to what you were taught about the world up to about 7 years old. And how do these early lessons affect your expectations about the world today?

The wondering years

1. What are three of your biggest and most important memories that, as far as you can recall, happened before the age of 7? Take your time, they are there somewhere.

2. What did these memories teach you?

3. What did these memories make important to you that is still true today e.g. love, connection, honesty, security?

It is often surprising to find just how much those early experiences of love, connection and security still affect us today. These memories are part of your deepest 'programming'.

I wonder what you at 7 years old would say if you showed them your list of dreams now? What would they tell you to do next?

These years of learning lay the foundations but then, as you reach 7 years old or thereabouts, your mind begins to change and your filters refocus on a new type of 'normal'.

WHO'S NORMAL IS IT ANYWAY?

Here is the easiest way for me to prove how your mind changes as you get that little bit older; think back to being about 9 years old. Do you remember any early thoughts of really wanting to be or do something when you got older? I'm guessing that by then you no longer wanted to be a superhero, magical princess or a cat (most people anyway!).

Somewhere around 7 or 8, you began looking at the world around you, decided what looked good/fun/exciting/interesting and started to work out how you could get a piece of it. Maybe you wanted to go to space (but no longer dream of being the actual rocket!), be a champion in your favourite sport, be rich, famous, successful or, very commonly, you saw someone do something amazing on TV, in a film or on the internet and decided that was definitely the future for you.

My own personal memory is of an insatiable desire to be a tap dancer! This dancing passion faded at about age 11, but more on that in a minute. . . .

At this age you were excited by possibilities and opportunities. Your mind, for the first time, was under *your* control however, at least at the beginning of this period, you still held onto a little bit of that childlike belief that life could deliver anything if you wanted it badly enough.

From age 7 up to about 14, you start to pay attention to a range of people who seem to have the life you want; family members, celebrities, friends, friend's family members, coaches, musicians, teachers, and virtually anyone that inspires you has the opportunity to become a role model for you in some area of your life.

Like a colourful collage, you begin to design the life you want simply because you want it. There is no thought of rules, goals or what needs to be done to make that life happen. At this stage you are simply trying things on. Like a magic box of emotional costumes, you play and practise with the feelings these people give you, slowly discovering and developing what feels best to you.

Perhaps one of your role models shows you how a loving relationship should be, perhaps another shows you a spiritual path, another shows you the meaning of financial success, another shows you the car you would like to drive when you get older, another teaches you about a particular subject you will love all your life, another shows you exactly who you don't want to be.

And that's also important to know.

Some people will become 'anti-role models'. They show you exactly what you *don't* want to do or how you *don't* want to be. You will have met these people in your life. We all have.

Perhaps someone causes us physical, emotional or mental pain or perhaps someone causes themselves pain. Whichever it is, our negative, anti-role models can often steer our lives even more powerfully than our positive ones. Pain, as we discussed way back in Chapter 1 is a powerful, if not particularly pleasant, motivator.

The pain they cause us (or themselves) can become a permanent driver of our character, pushing us to be bigger, better and more driven to success than they ever were. In fact, just as we need role models to teach us who we want to be, perhaps each and every one of us *needs* an anti-model to teach us who we *don't* want to be.

Whichever way they go, the role models and anti-models you pick up before about age 14 will have an influence that will stay with you for the rest of your life. Each and every person you encounter during this period of your life has the opportunity to make a huge and lasting impact on you.

This is really important to understand, especially if you are over the age of 21. Every time you meet someone between the ages of about 7 and 14 you have the potential to significantly shape their life.

Remember to ask yourself which type of role model you want to be.

But let's get back to growing up. . . .

It will have been during this time, as you raced up on early adulthood, that you started putting posters on your wall, developing your first proper crush, becoming obsessed with people or things, making some of your earliest decisions about your future and, again, you did all of this based on the actions of what you saw around you in the world.

But of course, your thoughts of what was possible were still most affected by those closest to you.

For example, imagine a 10 year old girl wants to be an astronaut. In one reality she is supported, encouraged and guided by a supporting cast of many, especially her parents. She is inspired and excited about space and given every opportunity to learn.

In another reality, she is told to stop being silly, to concentrate on something more realistic, ridiculed for her crazy ideas and told 'girls like you don't go to space'. She is held back from being curious and taught that passion must be realistic (whatever that means).

In which reality will it be easier for her to find the motivation to succeed and achieve her dream?

The influence of the people who surround you in your early years begins to fade in the time period from about age 7 to about 14. I imagine it like someone slowly turning down the volume on their ability to cause ripples in our world.

The volume can decrease so much that, when you hit 14, those bonds may loosen completely. But it is more common to find that some linger and continue to influence your decisions. By the time you reach 14 you will likely have established life long role models that will still be affecting your decisions to this day.

Here is a really short exercise in gratitude. Sometimes it's easy to get so consumed with just getting on with life that we never look back. It can be a powerful and emotional experience to take the time to say 'thank you' to those people that made us who we are, even if it's not possible to say it in person.

We could be heroes

1. Who did you look up to when you were growing up?

2. What specifically did you learn from them?

3. Would they be proud of what you have achieved?

4. What advice would they have for you today?

5. What would you say to them if you could?

As you grow up, it is as you reach age 14 or thereabouts when it's time for you to finally decide for yourself where your life is heading and who you want to be. It's at this stage that your future really begins to take shape.

TRIBAL MARKINGS

The unstoppable march to adulthood is nearing completion and your mind must go through one final significant learning shift.

Amongst all the noise, a question will bubble up to the forefront of your mind and will get louder and louder until you are about 21. That question?

How do I fit in?

After 14 years of allowing other people to guide your life, you now have the chance to make a path for yourself. Your mind begins to break free from childhood and make its own decisions.

You begin to exercise your right to reject the rules and ideas of everyone you've grown up with and you start to replace as many of these as you can with a whole new set of your own.

Green hair, piercings, tattoos, music your parents don't understand, friends they don't approve of, experiments with drink, drugs and sex, and fashion choices that you will probably reflect on in years to come and regret. These are all a necessary rite of passage through a critical period of growth.

And as you make all of these dodgy choices, the most important thing to you is that the choice is totally and completely *yours*! You can do what you want. You are finally your own person.

Or are you?

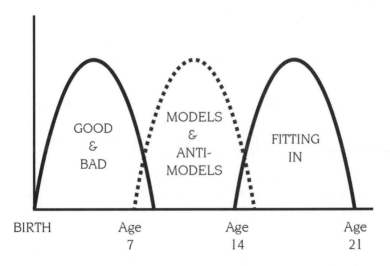

Think about yourself between the ages of about 14 and 17, right at the beginning of this stage.

How did you respond to the new found freedom your mind was enjoying? Did you rebel? Did you conform? Did you retreat inside a shell? Did you act out? Did you explode in a multi coloured shower of hair dye and ripped clothes?

Well, whatever you did I have a question for you. Why? Why did you do the things you did?

Usually the beginning of this period is defined by what your friends and the rest of your 'tribe' (i.e. the social peer group you are most attracted to) are doing and thinking. If they have green hair, you want green hair. If they think people with green hair are weird, you think people with green hair are weird.

During this period, we are getting used to the concept of adulthood and individuality. However, most of us find safety and certainty in groups and, because we are part of a group, we give ourselves permission to push the boundaries of what we believe is acceptable. It feels exciting while, at exactly the same time, it also feels safe.

Although we tell the world we're being individual, we tend to be individual within a group of friends who are all the same as us! It's like the ultimate emotional roller coaster . . . would you ever go on a roller coaster if it looked like some of the safety equipment wasn't working? Of course not. We enjoy these thrill rides because they give us a totally safe way to experience the illusion of risk. They are 'safe danger'.

This is what our 'tribe' gives us.

As teenagers we are still playing, its just that now we are playing at being grown ups. It is the human equivalent of maturing lion cubs learning how to hunt by grabbing each other in head locks, or the impala fawn who learns to escape the lion by running around in a dance.

We 'play' with all our firsts; first love, first heartbreak, first job, first real money, first exams, first successes, first failures, first time away from home, first drink, first smoke. If we like it we do it more, if we don't like it we stop it. Simple.

This is your mind pushing the boundaries of what you believe is possible, to discover who you could be.

Have you seen the programme Dragons Den where entrepreneurs and inventors bring products to wealthy investors and 'bid' for money to take their product or service to the next level and make them rich? In the UK version of the show, there was one particular millionaire investor who was famous for taking various products and bending them, pulling and twisting them to check the build quality. Many, many products failed this test and ended up in bits and he never invested in a product that failed to withstand his physical stress testing.

Well, this is exactly what you are doing to life as you mature through your teens. You are testing your emotional range to see how far you can push it before it breaks. That's why you take so many crazy risks and make so many daft decisions when you are this age, you want to see just what sort of 'stress testing' life can take as you push the boundaries.

That said, everyone has their own idea of what constitutes 'risk' and pushing the boundaries has different meaning for different people. For every teenager who gets a full face spider web tattoo there is another who decides to only study in the library two nights a week instead of four.

The influence of your parents, or whoever looked after you in your early years, has faded by this stage as you move closer and closer to leaving the security of the family environment and going out on your own. It may not disappear completely but it will be weaker than before.

But even as you go out on your own, you will never stop learning from others. You will always have role models although their pedestal definitely gets lower as you get older. You are establishing your own identity, your own model of the world, and to do that you must take risks, push boundaries and make mistakes!!

So to summarise . . . from about 14 to about 21 almost everything we do is practice. If we allow ourselves, even on reflection, the freedom to fail we also allow ourselves the freedom to surprise ourselves. Reflect back and look for the lessons (embarrassing as they may be!) rather than that bad haircut or those spectacular hangovers.

Scream if you want to go faster

1. Between the ages of about 14 and 21, what did you do to fit in?

2. What did you do at this age that, looking back, makes you question your fashion sense/personal values/sanity?

3. Why did you do those things? What did you get from them at the time?

4. What did you learn from them that still applies today?

We tend to ignore those teenage years, seeing them as a wasteland of bad decisions but actually, many of the lessons you learned at that time about who you are and what you like, will still be affecting you today.

SETTLING INTO NORMALITY

So, you have now constructed a map of 'normal' over 21 years of trial and error, role models and anti-models, experimentation, listening and learning, being guided and supported. This map will, for the rest of your life, tell you how life *should* be.

Now, it is really important to know that this map of your 'normal' will always be open to change. We are not (much as some may wish to be) 21 forever and things have to change to allow us to grow and evolve.

We picked out the first 21 years because they are the most active, fast moving and open when it comes to change. As we grow older, any Big Bang or Drip Feed experience can alter the map, sometimes permanently. For example, it doesn't matter what age you are, if you meet the person of your dreams, fall head over heels in love and move into the same house as them, that experience will change you.

Why? Because if you are motivated to fall in love and want to share your carefully constructed map of 'normal life' with another person, then that person must be giving you the feelings you want. They must be 'ticking the boxes' of your internal motivational 'code'.

If you can learn to be aware of this 'code' and how it is programmed, you will have access to the key that unlocks the deepest motivating forces of your mind.

That sounds pretty cool doesn't it?

Oh, there's only one slight issue though . . . your mind knows how this code is programmed, but it's keeping it a secret!

CRACKING THE CODE

Well, not so much keeping it a secret as keeping it hidden. You see, your code to motivation is written in emotions and emotions are tough to spot when you are having an amazing time being motivated!

I mean, when you are in a great relationship and everything is going fab, do you ever take the time to stop and ask yourself, in any particular moment, why you are feeling so good? When your career is kicking ass and you love what you do, do you ever sit back in your chair on a break and think about the emotions you are feeling at that time and make a note of remembering them in case you ever need them in the future?

In fact, in both of these simple examples, if you were to ask someone why they are feeling so amazing, many people will put all their motivation down to someone or something else saying, 'I feel great because he/she just makes me feel so happy'. Or they will put it down to luck saying, 'I don't know what it is, things just seem really good at the moment' when actually what they've done is unlock a deep, unconscious, emotional code that it has taken their whole lifetime to that point to write.

Let me ask you just one simple question right now so that you can discover a small portion of your own code. This exercise is much easier to do if you write the answers down in your notebook or on a piece of paper but if you don't feel motivated to do that then that's fine too!

Revealing the code

Write down at least five (no more than ten) of the most important things you need to feel in a relationship? (e.g. security, love, freedom, romance, happiness, independence, intimacy or any other feeling you can think of)

Now, I bet you would find it quite straightforward to go back over all of those feelings and tell me why each is important to you in a relationship. It's important to note that each of these words will have a meaning that is unique to you and you will have your own reasons for choosing them.

You may remember a specific lesson you learned that led to you marking that particular feeling as a vital component in your version of a good relationship. For example, anyone who has ever been cheated on (there's a perfect example of a Big Bang moment by the way) will almost definitely have 'trust' somewhere on their list of what's important to them in a relationship.

However, the practical meaning of 'trust' can vary from one person to the next. One person might show trust in a relationship by leaving their partner to their own hobbies and friends and not butting in while, to someone else, trust means being able to pick their partner's phone up at any time and read all their messages. We'll come back to this concept in a minute.

Whatever your own interpretation of these feelings (which can also be called *values*) may be, together they make up your own individual code for relationships. You also have a hierarchy of codes inside you that will unlock motivation for the other areas of your life – family, work, friends, finances, etc.

Your life is *entirely* defined by the values that make up your code and it is this code that you use to make ALL your decisions.

The clothes you wear, the friends you have, the relationship you are (or are not) currently enjoying, your favourite movies, music and TV, the car you drive, the things you like to do at the weekend, your job, the colour of your duvet cover, the contents of your fridge, your weight, your hairstyle, your financial situation, if you are late or early for a meeting, where you like to shop, etc, etc. All of these aspects of your life and every other decision you will ever make are defined by your internal emotional code.

Have I stressed that enough?

Every decision.

That means every single negative emotion you have ever felt in your life has been due to something in your code either not being met or being violated. We have established that the sole intention of your mind is to make you feel great, so when it is presented with something that doesn't fit or is the opposite of what you want then of course it is going to give you some pain to get you back on track!

If you have strong values for safety, security and control and then all of a sudden something comes along and totally rocks your world, e.g. you are made redundant, then you are going to feel fear and anxiety. That's pretty much guaranteed but it's not because your mind wants to hurt you, actually the total opposite. Your mind is simply sensing danger and trying anything it can to quickly motivate you to do something to get back to safety, security and control.

Does that make sense?

Anxiety isn't a bad part of your mind trying to scare the bejesus out of you! In fact, anxiety is always about protection and safety. Your mind perceives danger and wants you to run away. And remember, as you learned back in chapter 2, that danger doesn't even have to be real – your mind will always respond to an imagined danger as if it was 100% real.

Let's look at depression as an example. Depression isn't a broken connection that means you can never be happy again. In most cases, depression is about having too many 'shoulds' in your life and feeling overwhelmed by the things you are not doing or don't have. And how do you know you want to do those things or that you want those things? Yep, it's your code again. Your mind is sad and overwhelmed by the distance it has between where it is now and where it thinks it *should* be, it's just showing you an ideal life that will match your internal code. Your mind wants you to have it so it is constantly comparing your version of 'normal' to what is actually going on. The further apart those two are, the more overwhelmed you are going to feel.

That's not broken, that's working perfectly!!

Your mind is never trying to hurt you with negative emotions. Your mind is the best, closest and most trusted friend you have. But it isn't taking any of your crap. If you are doing or experiencing something that doesn't fit the code then it is going to hurt you until you change either the situation itself or your thoughts about it.

It's a bit like the concept of 'dark'.

Did you know that, scientifically speaking, 'dark' does not exist? If you look outside your house at 1am on a winter's night, sorry to tell you, that isn't dark you are seeing. Put yourself in a cupboard with no window and close the door? That isn't dark either. When you think you are experiencing darkness, what you are actually experiencing is an absence of light. In science, there is no such thing as dark, only places that light can't reach.

And here we are at the crux of many of the emotional issues that plague us today.

Depression, anxiety, anger, stress – all these feelings are simply an absence of the positive. They aren't necessarily an illness and you definitely aren't broken beyond repair. They are manifestations of *negative motivation*. Your mind is trying to motivate you back in the direction of something better by making you hurt.

Your mind is giving you a hard kick up the arse and looking for you to make decisions. It's up to you how many times you are going to let it kick you before you do what's necessary!

Here's the last exercise for this chapter. It's easy to get caught up in the fantasy that your whole life is in turmoil when actually you are being 'kicked' for something specific. The image over the page provides a rough idea of what a simple map of life could look like.

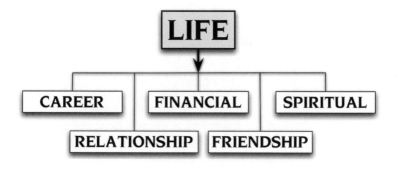

Imagine the big chunky 'LIFE' box contains everything this person wants for a fulfilled and happy life, followed by the five big significant areas of life. Each of these areas will have its own emotional code and each has the potential to be vastly different from the others. For example, someone who needs security in their career can easily demand independence in their relationship. As we have covered, the code all depends on the experiences of the Big Bangs and Drip Feeds and how they have guided this person to this point in their life.

I promise, it is rare (although not impossible) to find someone who has ended up with every single one of these areas being a disaster. It is much more common to find one area that is causing the most problems. Let's do a quick exercise to illustrate this point. This one can easily be done in your head but please feel free to write it out if you want to.

Shrinking the problems

1. Rate each of the life areas shown in the diagram on the previous page out of 10, where 10 means it is going better than you could ever have imagined and a 1 means it is a total disaster.

2. When you're done, look at the scores you have given for each area. This is a rough guide to what they mean:
   - 10 = Fantastic, no problems.
   - 7–9 = Excellent and going well.
   - 4–6 = Going OK, maybe wee things could be better.
   - 1–3 = Uh-oh, needs some real attention to make it better.

3. For anything rated 7 or above, congratulate yourself and take time to notice what you do that makes this work.

4. For anything rated 4–6, if you could change one simple thing that would move the score up just one point, what would that be?

5. For anything rated 1–3, be honest about what it is that you are not doing right now to make it better. If you were to make one simple (but potentially huge) decision today that would change it and raise the rating, what would it be?

6. Go change what needs to be changed!

This can be an enlightening exercise. It's easy to complain about how your life is a total mess when actually it isn't. It's just that you aren't making the key decisions that you need to make to move out of a place that isn't serving you.

How many people do you know who are in a job they hate, a relationship that is finished or hanging around with friends who hurt them but they don't do anything to change these situations?

The hate, hurt and apathy is the code not being served or, even worse, being violated. Your mind is giving you pain to show you that what you are doing is not working.

Remember, it doesn't want to hurt you. You are not broken. It is a messenger, a teacher and a guide.

But then we experience a new problem. If you don't know your code then how can you possibly make sure you are meeting it?

When you feel depressed, how can you move back towards what you want if you have no idea what that actually is? Is it safety? Love? Happiness? Something else entirely?

As I said right at the beginning of this chapter, life is not about luck or fate. Life can be about design. But to harness the power to design your life you need to do something huge.

You need to realise you are not who you think you are.

Chapter 4 in a nutshell:

- Motivation is not a feeling. You need to *get* motivated, not feel motivated.

- Motivation is driven by an internal code that we have taught ourselves through the pleasure and pain of experience.

- Your code, like your rules, is not 'right' or 'wrong', it is only useful or not useful.

- Every single thing you do is driven by a positive intention. Even the crazy stuff. Yes, really!

- Decipher your code by asking 'what is my mind trying to get me right now' and look for the positive behind every action.

Doing the right thing – revisited

We have a tendency to refer to our emotions as nouns when actually they are verbs i.e. whether it's happiness, sadness, confidence or fear, emotions are not something you have, they are something you do. As we return to Declan's story, let's focus on confidence.

Because emotions are something you do, you can't be given confidence, you can't lose or gain confidence, you can't give confidence to someone else and you definitely can't be born with more than anyone else. You see, Declan hadn't lost his confidence; he had actually found a way to stop himself feeling it. And the answer lay deep in his 'code'.

I asked him about the code he used to navigate his career and we examined the unconscious feelings he used to make decisions in his job. As soon as he identified the feeling of 'doing the right thing', we both realised it was massively important. In fact, just in saying those words out loud, the words he had been hearing in his mind for so long, he actually began to feel the negative emotions that he felt at work.

We traced this back to the Big Bang moment – ironically a promotion at his old job two years before he was made redundant. He found himself in a position for which he was neither prepared nor properly trained and was left to sink or swim. He sank. There followed a daily Drip Feed of anxiety as he battled not to make a mistake. Every day he was super careful to make sure he always tried to *do the right thing*.

That part of his code became so ingrained that it didn't matter that everything else changed in the new job. Because the code isn't part of the job, it's part of Declan so he was still too anxious to make a decision just in case he didn't 'do the right thing'.

Your code is created through experiences and is never fixed. Declan and I spent the rest of our session ensuring that the negative emotions of the past were left behind and no longer affected his present and future. Lessons were learned, confidence returned and the new job started to go a hell of a lot better!

Once you realise how you are holding yourself back, change will happen easily.

Sometimes the only person getting in the way of your success and your happiness is *you*.

Who's bubble is the right bubble?

A few years ago I was delivering a Breakthrough Weekend course when a most bizarre set of circumstances arose.

We finished up the first day of the course and everything had gone really well. Everyone was up for it, the atmosphere in the room was fantastic and the rapport between the participants was excellent. All the ingredients for an awesome weekend of transformations!

As the course was being held locally I was relaxing at home later that evening when my phone rang at about 9pm. I don't know what made me answer it as normally I like to clear my head, reconnect with the family and mentally prepare for the second day. But this time, for some reason I did and I was puzzled to hear a lady introduce herself as Erin's mum.

Erin was one of our delegates from the course that day, a lovely bubbly girl who had just turned 20. Mum sounded a little anxious as she asked if I knew where Erin had gone after the course and if I had, for some reason, heard from her.

I hadn't but I had noticed that she had hit it off with a couple of the other younger delegates. With it being Glasgow on a Saturday night and they'd had great fun on the course, I ventured a wild guess that they might be in a local hostelry!

I offered to contact one of the other delegates to see if Erin was with them. I did that but didn't hear anything back. At least until the morning of the second day!

As I approached the training room the next morning, Erin ran up to me apologising profusely for her mum's call the night before. She was very angry at her mum's behaviour and described how she had gone to the pub for a couple of drinks, accidentally left her phone on silent and, when I had contacted one of the group to ask her to call home and she finally looked at her phone she had 34 missed calls, 19 texts and Dad was out driving the streets looking for her. She was two hours late home.

"Why does she keep treating me like a child? She is just always on me. I'm 20 years old and my mum is phoning people she doesn't even know to chase me home when I'm out with friends." This was just part of her rant – I could empathise with her and understand her frustration.

It was clear to see how much her mum's behaviour had upset her and I could imagine what it must be like to be 20, have all the responsibilities of adulthood and still have your mum worry and chase around after you when you're not home on time.

But importantly I also understood why her mum was worried and why she did what she did. Of course at this stage of the course, Erin hadn't yet learned that she too could have that insight.

5

The conscious witness

Do you find that it's easier to give someone else advice on their problems than to sort out your own? How many times have you found yourself giving someone advice when you realise that you should really be listening to that advice yourself?

Ever wondered why that happens?

Why is it that good advice flows so easily when we aim it at someone else yet it feels so sticky and difficult when we try to apply it to ourselves? How is it our mind works so damn effortlessly when it's not our own problem we're sorting out? Could it really be simply down to our thoughts and perceptions again?

There are three ways to look at the world around you. You can look at it as 'You', you can see it through the eyes of 'Them', i.e. someone that isn't you, or you can be a 'Witness', looking on like a fly on the wall, a neutral observer.

These three different ways of perceiving the world will each have an instant and profound effect on how you behave. You already know that of course because you now understand,

Thought = Feeling = Action

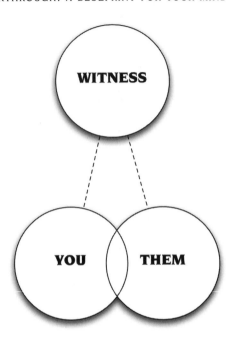

In case you need a quick reminder . . . you are who you are because you live inside a bubble. You have a unique and special bubble (you probably call it your mind) which acts like a big filter on the outside world, ignoring and twisting all the information it receives to make sure it matches your internal assumptions about what 'normal' is like. Your mind knows how to do this based on a set of rules that you have established through a whole lifetime of experiences up to this point in your life right now. These rules are designed to assist you in guiding your life experiences to match a specific, deeply held emotional 'code' that will lead you to motivation and ultimate happiness.

But what if it is possible to change the filter through which you view life and think with a whole new set of rules and a whole new code in an instant? What if one simple change of perception could give you access to resources, skills and ideas you don't even know you possess? What if you stepped into someone else's bubble and started to see the world the way they do? What if you are already doing this and you've just not noticed yet?!

Remember, there are three useful ways to perceive the world around you. . . .

PLAYING WITH YOURSELF

The first one is the most obvious yet it is also the one that many people find the most difficult to put into action.

Simply being *you*.

Here's a quick exercise for you to do in your head or write down. I promise it will take no more than 20 seconds. Go with your first answers before the filters kick in and keep going until you have five.

Removing the mask

What are the first five things that come to mind if I ask 'Who are you?'

Now, how many of these five things would you be proud to be known for? If your time on this earth was suddenly up tomorrow, would you be happy to be remembered for these things? Or do you feel that your list has some rather underwhelming, uninspiring attributes such as your job, the fact you are a careful person or that you like hamsters?

Whatever your answer, I promise there is more to who you are than you are currently willing to admit. In reality, everyone's list is far longer than just five, including yours.

For many people, there are aspects of our life, our experiences and our achievements that we are proud of but we don't tell people because we are worried about what they might think. I bet there are aspects of your life that mean a lot to you but you didn't put them on your list because 'it's not really that important' or 'it's just a small thing, nothing special'?

How would your life change if every decision you make from this day forward was made to fit in with *your own* emotional code no matter what happens? Sometimes, as the old saying goes, you have to look after number one and there's an easy way to check how good you are at just being 'you'. Ask yourself two simple questions,

1. How many times do you change your mind because you want to make or keep someone else happy?

2. And how many times do you hold yourself back from doing what you want because you worry about what other people will think or feel about it?

I'm not suggesting that being totally selfish in all aspects of life is the way forward either! As we will discuss later, there are times where we need to be selfish and other times where we need to put others first. Life is, amongst many other things, all about balance. But a happy life, a fulfilled life, a successful life demands the ability to make big decisions. Look around and you'll find all happy, fulfilled, successful people have an ability to make big decisions on their own.

For example, if you are the leader of a team, you can't possibly run every decision by every member of your team to check that they are all OK with it. Leadership is not a community based activity! The best leaders will be able to assess the situation, take it inside their bubble, be decisive about the action that they feel is best and, most importantly, handle the consequences.

**The quality of your life is directly related
to your ability to make decisions.**

Almost all cultures, societies and businesses value decision making highly and are willing to pay a lot of money to people who are good at it! The decision makers will always get promoted, noticed, even admired because in that crunch moment they can do what many others can't do. They *act*.

To move forward in life, you have to start making decisions!

This next exercise is about building up your decision making 'muscle'. Just like any other muscle in your body, you need to exercise and get 'decision fit'. That means pushing yourself to do things you wouldn't normally do.

As you do this exercise, write down the decisions you commit to making. You will forget them if you try and keep them all in your head, so write them down. The decisions you commit to make should all stretch you and be something that you would normally find difficult but they don't need to be significantly life changing.

If you start too big you'll freak yourself out, give up and go back to how it was before. You would never think about going to the gym for the first time and starting on the big boy weights in the corner would you?

When this exercise asks you to make 'small' decisions, it really means it, so make a decision about what the family has for dinner, or which movie you are going to watch or what you are going to wear (remember, all without asking anyone if it is ok with them).

Decide to decide

1. Where are you already confident at making your own decisions?

2. Write down three *small* decisions you can make *today* that will make you happy.

3. How could those decisions go wrong?

4. And what would happen if they did?

5. Repeat Steps 2–4 but this time make it three decisions you can make this week.

6. Do it again but this time it's three decisions you can make in the next month.

My recommendation is that you make this exercise a regular part of your morning routine, asking yourself 'What can I decide today?'

I guarantee that you will be amazed at just how quickly you become more decisive and start living the life you want to live.

And the most important bit . . . make sure you see those decisions through to the end! There is no change without action.

However, you also need to be aware that, if left unchecked, there is a downside to making decisions based purely on what you want. If you are not careful then you will very soon have no friends!

Have you ever met someone who uses the excuse 'I was only being myself' as permission to be a prize-wining idiot? Everything they do and say is designed to meet their needs, their code, their rules and they don't seem able to notice that other people may not like it, or even that they may be hurting others. They fully expect that their behaviour, even if it's anti-social or rude can be forgiven by claiming that no-one can argue with their personal code.

And in one regard they are right. As we established in chapter 4, it is actually true that no-one can argue with a person's personal code. It has taken a lifetime to write and is constantly being changed to keep that person on the path to happiness and peace. But just because it can't be argued with, doesn't mean everyone else will like it!

And there lies a problem, if you connect too much to *you*, you can become disconnected from *them* (whoever they may be). If you really want to make the most of your life, other people are important, so it is an incredibly useful skill to be able to climb out of your bubble and drop, for a time, into . . .

SOMEONE ELSE'S SHOES

How many times a day to you try and read someone else's mind?

If you answered less than ten then you are either a hermit or a liar!

One of the most useful skills your mind learns as you grow up is the ability to guess the thoughts and actions of other people. Every single day your mind makes judgments, forecasts and assumptions about what is happening in other people's minds so that you can successfully move through the world. Some of these guesses may be more successful than others and some people may be better at it than others, but we all do it all the time.

For example, how many times have you walked away from a conversation and wondered about what was being said after you left, or indeed before you arrived?

How many times have you had a conversation and known exactly how the other person was going to respond or what they were going to say before they said it?

How many times do you have fantasy conversations (and/or arguments) with other people inside your mind or even out loud only for that conversation to never, ever happen?

If you have ever done any of these things, your mind is trying to 'read' the thoughts and actions of someone else. And that's pretty cool but if that is as far as you go with this particular ability then you are only using a tiny portion of its real power. You see, many people never stop thinking about themselves for long enough to use this skill to its full potential.

Not you though. Well not any more, anyway! Let me explain. . . .

What we are really doing when we 'step into someone's shoes' is making decisions about the intentions of their thoughts. This is not easy to do – it takes a high level of awareness to completely climb out of your own judgments and see the world through the other person's eyes.

For instance, we all have someone in our world who has hurt us or caused us pain. If a friend was to ask you why this person did the things they did, what would you say? Would you say it was because they are just nasty, or angry, or damaged? As we discussed earlier, our natural reaction is to judge others by their behaviours and ourselves by our intentions. So it follows that you will make a judgment of the other person based on how their behaviour made you feel and not on what their intention may have been.

Even if by chance your judgment of the other person based on how you feel happens to be right, you should ask if that judgment helps you in any way or does it just keep you stuck running painful memories? I think you know which answer is more likely.

So now let's flip it. If I asked the person who hurt you for *their* perspective on whatever they did do you think they would say *they* were nasty, angry or damaged? I think you'll agree its unlikely. They might call their actions defensive, decisive, honest, maybe even protective, but I guarantee you they would not call themselves any of the names you called them!

If you can train yourself to see behind the behaviours of others, to realise that ultimately everyone is looking out for themselves, you will find yourself in a place of significant influence over the people around you. One result of this will often be success in the social aspects of life because, not only can you tell what people want, you know how to help them get it.

When you become a skilled 'bubble jumper' (this is a new term I just made up . . . roll with it), you will fully understand the code of the other person in any interaction. You will have the ability to effortlessly alter your communication style to match their code without ever compromising your own, always staying entirely 'you'.

I remember coaching a client, let's call her Laura, through a significant conflict with a work colleague who we'll call Susan. Laura found Susan to be unpleasant, awkward and annoying and was actually planning to transfer to another team just to get away from her. That was the view from Laura's bubble.

However, when I taught Laura to 'bubble jump' and see the world through Susan's 'eyes', she discovered a colleague who had recently returned from a long-term absence through ill health, returning to a vastly different team from the one she had left. Two or three gentle guiding questions later, and Laura began to cry as it became clear that Susan wasn't really being awkward and she definitely didn't want to upset anyone. In fact, the true situation was almost the exact opposite.

When we took the time to jump into Susan's world, Laura could appreciate the high levels of anxiety her colleague was experiencing. Many changes had been implemented while Susan had been ill including new team members, unfamiliar systems and new roles. These, together with her struggle to recover from her illness and, ironically, how her colleagues perceived that illness, had combined to leave Susan struggling to fit into the fast paced work environment.

This transformation in her perception, had almost instantly defused the whole situation for Laura. She had now changed how she thought about the situation . . . and you know what happens when you change your thoughts. She and Susan even became close friends!

Here's the process I used to guide Laura. It looks like a lot in the box but in reality it only takes 5 minutes. To make this work, you need to answer the questions from the perspective of being in a situation of conflict with another person. To start with, answer the questions as you.

Bubble jumping

1. How are you feeling when this conflict is happening?

2. How are you behaving when this conflict is happening.

3. How do you think the other person is feeling while this conflict is happening?

4. How are they behaving while this conflict is happening?

5. What do you want to achieve by doing what you are doing?

6. What do you wish the other person would realise?

   Now, go back through the questions, but do it from the perspective of the other person. Make sure that you are seeing the world as they do, their experiences, their position, their bubble.

7. What's the biggest insight you have gained from this exercise?

There is another section to this exercise that we will come back to later, but I hope that whatever the example of conflict that you chose, you have at least softened your view on the situation. As I say to everyone I take through this exercise, what we're looking for here is clarity and insight, not necessarily a life change. If you get a life change though, take it!

READING MINDS

There is often a challenge here, and you may have experienced it during that last exercise; how can you, or anyone else, really know what another person is thinking? Am I suggesting that we tap into some kind of universal subconscious and use it to read minds?

In short, no, I'm not. Because that would be silly!

As we know, our whole world is based on nothing more than perception and this must also include other people.

You have never known, and will never know, the whole of anyone. You may come close with your partner, closest friends and members of your family but there will always be moments when the people closest to you surprise you and do things you don't expect. This is because your perception of them is ultimately limited (as is their perception of you). Every relationship you have ever had, whether you remember it as a loving one or something else entirely, is a relationship you had with your perception of the other person.

Jumping into someone else's bubble is about you accessing, as fully and completely as you can, *your perception* of how that person thinks or feels. You will never know if you are right unless you ask them but you can make a really good guess. And that guess is often enough to change how you think, which will, in turn, change how you feel and change how you act.

Now, are you ready to understand the brain scrambling bit?

Changing how *you* think, feel and act is often enough to radically change a relationship because then, in *their* perception, you are no longer the trigger that you once were. This in turn, must change *their* thoughts, and feelings and then *they* act differently towards you. This means that they are no longer the trigger they once were to *you* which will change how *you* think and feel which will change . . . [and repeat].

Do you get the idea?

This applies to any time you are with other human beings.

If you are a teacher, a trainer or presenter, you should spend time being your audience. What do they want to hear? What do they need? A poor public speaker says what they want to say, a great public speaker says what they want to say in a way their audience wants to hear and delivers a useful message.

If you are a parent, how do your children perceive you? How do they perceive your relationship? How do they perceive the things you do? What code are you teaching them?

If you are a manager or leader, what do the people you lead need and want? Have you ever taken the time to think about what your team's perception is of you?

If your children, your team and everyone else in your life are usually motivated by either pleasure or pain, which do they associate with you?

Sitting on top of your world

Being good at bubble jumping is a fantastic skill that you can use to significantly improve your life, but there is a downside. Trying to make a decision from inside someone else's bubble is almost impossible – be empathic but be aware that, if you are *too* empathic, you can paralyse your decision-making ability.

Earlier in this chapter we concluded that a manager who seeks the approval of every team member before they make any decision will not be the manager for very long!

Similarly, as you work to master bubble jumping, you should guard against becoming stuck in everyone else's bubble.

It's a matter of priorities.

Just two simple questions will reveal where you rank yourself in the priorities of your life;

1. Who is first in your life?

2. Did you answer "I am"?

We all know people who do amazing things for others. These people want to do the right thing, make the big difference, help people, heal the world, but many of them are running on empty and don't actually have anything left to give.

Many of the most caring people I have ever met were so busy looking after everyone else and helping them achieve happiness that they were losing a bit of themselves and even sacrificing their own happiness. This is in contrast to all of the happiest and most successful[1] people I have ever met who know how to look after others *and* themselves at the same time. The classic win-win.

---

[1] Success is a completely subjective concept and not, as the media or the National Lottery may want you to believe, necessarily linked to financial wealth!

It's all about finding balance.

If *you* want to be happy, you need to be at the very top of *your* priority list. Every decision you make needs to be good for you, i.e. satisfy the needs of your own code first and put everyone else second.

For many people, the idea of putting themselves first, especially in front of their kids, is completely alien and utterly selfish, but I would ask you to challenge that belief. Imagine if you could live your life by your code and you are happy. How can anyone ever say that is selfish?

You can never be truly happy through sacrifice alone. It is certainly a noble and good thing to help other people but you simply cannot give what you do not have. If you are running low on energy then how can you give energy to others? If you don't feel happy then how can you give happiness to others? If you can't let yourself feel loved then how can you give love to others?

Would you take advice on losing weight from an overweight slimming coach? Would you take a hypnotherapist seriously if they told you that their 2-hour stop smoking plan was guaranteed while taking a deep drag on their cigarette? If not, then why would anyone accept love and care from someone that cannot love and care for themselves?

The most important person in your life must always be you.

Let's have a look at how much time you spend thinking about what other people think. This can easily be done in your head but, as you have already learned, there is extra power in writing it down. Be open and honest to get the most out of this exercise.

Freedom to choose

1. What are the three biggest decisions you would make in your own life today if you didn't care what other people thought of those decisions?

   Now ask yourself these questions about each decision individually:

2. Who specifically do you think you need permission from to make this decision?

3. Who do you know that would totally support you in making this decision? What would they say to you if you told them what you would love to do?

4. Who would complain about you making this decision? What would they say? Why would they say it (remembering what you have just learned about seeing it through their eyes)?

5. Putting everyone else's opinions aside, what would happen if you did make that decision now?

Before you go off and start making lots of changes in your life it's important to know I'm not advocating you just quit your job tomorrow without making plans for how you are going to eat and take care of the bills! Impulsive decisions are often just what you need to kick start a change in your life but it's important to balance impulse with reality.

Now that doesn't mean to say that you should delay making decisions to give yourself an excuse to say it can't happen either.

You just need to take a little time to time to make plans. Save what you need to save, sort out whatever needs to be sorted, do whatever you need to do. Just because it may not be the right decision to make now doesn't mean it's not the right decision to make.

And guess what? You even have a place in your mind you can go for a helping hand to make plans and get your ducks in a row. It's the place that finally answers the question about why it's easier to give someone else advice rather than take it yourself.

BEING THE WITNESS, NOT THE VICTIM

In yoga, there is a concept called Witness Consciousness, which lies at the very heart of yoga's spiritual discipline. Witness Consciousness is the deep understanding that you are not your thoughts or your mind. It is about accessing your spirit, your soul, your essence and realising that the body is merely a vessel that temporarily houses the real 'you'. This allows you to take a step back and realise that you are significantly more than the physical and material aspects of day-to-day life.

For a yogi (which, for the record, I am not!), achieving Witness Consciousness is considered the ultimate purpose of yoga practice and is a place that many yogis never achieve despite a lifetime of dedication and learning. I'm obviously not asking you to enter into years of spiritual and physical training, I just want you to think about the concept for a second – you are not your thoughts or your mind.

If you could step back from your life far enough to realise that your thoughts were simply illusions, how much freedom would it give you? Imagine being taken to a place where you can watch your life play back on a movie screen and be disconnected from it, watching it like a fly on the wall.

If you can imagine what that would be like, then you are becoming the witness.

This is why you find it easier to give other people advice that you should probably take for yourself. This is also why speaking your problems out loud or writing them down can sometimes make something that felt like the most serious thing in the world one minute, appear entirely ridiculous the next.

This is why people need therapists and coaches!

For the most part we are trapped in the illusion that our problems are real. If I have achieved anything in the writing of this book, I would love for you to have realised that this is not actually true. It is because I want you to experience the freedom of escaping this illusion that I keep emphasising our equation.

Thought = Feeling = Action

As we saw in chapter 2, if you can truly grasp that *everything* is perception, that nothing you are experiencing just now is real then you can tap into the power of your deepest internal processes rather than being caught up in them. You become a witness to your emotions rather than a victim of them.

The inside of your mind can often seem like an intriguing and bizarre place full of contradictions and confusion. I hope, by now, that you have figured out that it is actually very simple and all you have to do is take a step back and see it for what it really is – simple rules, adhering to a code made up of emotions.

And that's the joy of being a witness . . . it makes everything easier because it's no longer personal.

Want to see this in action? Think of a time when you've been annoyed at someone for more than a day or two but now everything is OK again. Got one? Don't worry, it's totally normal if your mind has just been flooded with examples – just pick one for now!

Now think about how hard you worked to stay annoyed at that other person for that long. How many angry conversations and arguments did you have with them inside your head? How many names did you call them? How many times were you totally sure you knew exactly what they were thinking, feeling and why they were acting they way they were?

How much energy did all that take?

And now that the argument and the anger have all blown over, how do you feel about how you acted, thought and behaved when you look back? Do you now feel that your actions were silly, stupid or over the top?

Well, guess what . . . they *were* silly, stupid and over the top!

The reason you can see your actions now for what they really were, when at the time they seemed totally justified, is that now you are viewing it all as a witness. You have become an onlooker to your own behaviour and noticed, from that place, that it was all a bit crazy!

It's so easy to get wrapped up in ourselves that we begin to believe that even someone doing something trivial like putting the ketchup in the cupboard rather than the fridge actually matters enough to stay angry for a day. In reality, all that matters is to keep life simple, free and happy.

Being the witness is about being objective and as much as is possible, removing the emotion from whatever you are 'witnessing', even if it is your own life you are looking at. As you practise this fly-on-the-wall perspective you begin to realise that all your responses and reactions are not 'real', they are learned cues that can change easily. Everyone has their own set and they are only real because we make them real.

If you are in a public place right now, take a minute or two to just watch the people around you. Notice how the world works and how people move through it.

Be a witness to everything that is happening around you right now.

Now, is anything you are watching impossible to change? Do you really believe that guy with the big headphones on couldn't do the same walk without them? Is it really impossible for that person screaming at the small child to deal with the situation in a calmer way?

But we treat all this as real. If this were happening to you instead of them, you would argue that this is the way it *has* to be.

But it doesn't.

Learning to be the witness is about learning to be outside your bubble which is exactly where you need to be to sort things out. Think about it, if you took the time to actually follow just 5% of the advice you give to others, your life would become increasingly sorted, wouldn't it?

So how do you do that? *How* do you actually become the witness?

I've actually already told you! In fact, the whole book has been about it!

Thought = Feeling = Action

Witness is the realisation that every action you will ever take is motivated by a feeling which is the result of a thought, a thought that you have learned to have.

Try it right now. This one doesn't need paper – just do it in your head. If you have time and want to really understand the power of this, it's worth doing it a few times.

Witnessing reality

1. Think about a challenge you are currently having in your life and notice how you view it inside your head.

2. Imagine 'stepping out' of the problem so that you can see yourself doing what you are doing when the problem is happening.

3. What advice would you give the version of 'you' that you are looking at?

This simple little routine is one of the most powerful change tools I have in my arsenal. If you can practise jumping out of your bubble, you are one step on the path towards achieving the Witness Consciousness we spoke about earlier.

So, with that in mind, I think the time has come to give you the big secret magic word that will sort out all of your issues and problems from now until forever.

If you'd like me to give you that magic word, you'll need to promise me that every time you feel *any* feeling you don't like, you are going to use this magic word.

Every single time.

Do we have a deal . . .?

Ok, so instead of getting wrapped up in the drama of all your feelings, you are now going to say,

"*Interesting . . .*"

And when you say this magic word, you are going to notice all the reasons your mind would choose to give you that particular feeling at that particular time.

So now it's time to finish the exercise we started earlier where we jumped between being You and Them in a situation that you are currently experiencing. It should be obvious where you are going next. . . .

Thinking about that conflict you worked with earlier, ask all these questions from the perspective of the Witness. Imagine looking into the conflict happening, almost like it was on TV (remember the magic word!).

Bubble jumping – the witness

1. How are the people in this conflict feeling?

2. How are they behaving at the key times in this conflict?

3. How are they each affecting the other?

4. What do you think both of them are trying to achieve?

5. What can you notice about this conflict that they can't see because they are too involved?

6. If you could give them some simple advice, what would it be?

In my experience, people who truly grasp the ethos of personal development have practised this ability to become their own witness over and over until it is completely second nature. To start with, it isn't easy to do. Like the yogis, it takes time, practice and attention but investing that time, practice and attention will pay dividends almost immediately. Try using the magic word and you'll see.

You'll also learn pretty quickly when it's right to use it and when it's not. In the heat of an argument or in the chaos of a really emotional moment, it is really difficult to be the witness. To be honest, in these moments you should just be you and not even try to be anywhere else. Your nearest and dearest don't want to argue, celebrate or, if I can be a little darker for a moment, mourn with someone who is detached from the situation and emotions. At these times you need to be emotional and connected and very much the exact opposite of the cold and detached witness.

Look at the way people often view senior management or politicians as uncaring, cold, unsympathetic, detached and unaware of what is really going on. This is the witness – would you like to think like a politician about every aspect of your relationship, life or career? I'm going to go ahead and assume that your answer is a resounding No!!

In actual fact, as we talked about earlier in this chapter, everything in life, including how we use our mind, is about balance. But what exactly does 'balance' mean?

SET PHASERS TO STUNNING

All of the mindsets we have learned in this chapter are fantastically useful if used appropriately. If you go too far, you get

Too much 'you' = selfish and uncaring
Too much 'them' = indecisive and paranoid
Too much 'witness' = cold and detached

And by the same logic, you don't want too *little* of any of them either!

My 'rule of thumb' is that for effortless day-to-day living, knowing how to be *You* and having the empathy to understand *Them* are the most essential skills and finding a balance between these two doesn't necessarily mean a 50/50 split. If you practise the decision making skills you have learned, live by your code, and never lose sight of those around you and how your decisions affect them, you will find your natural balance.

Every situation is different and every context can change the balance. Be open to making mistakes. Life is not about perfection, it's about doing the best you can. There is no exact science, no statistic to tell you what to do. You make the best decision for you at the time. Take charge or step back.

Balance.

If you look back, there will have been times when you haven't made the best decision for you, when you've allowed yourself to sacrifice your own needs and desires. You'll notice that it's these times from which almost all the pain in your life has come.

And then there's those moments when you made the big decision and did what you wanted to do, when you were honest with those around you and believed in yourself. Those will be the times you found pride and happiness. There is a clue in those examples as to how the balance should work!

And now the witness comes in. Think of the witness as being the 'balance checker'. A skilled witness can step back and give themselves advice on how to keep the balance. The witness is an observer, to guide, not to interfere.

Practise looking at your life from the outside. Give yourself a break from the chaos of 'doing' and take the time to become your own biggest supporter. Notice what you do, give yourself advice (and then take it). From this point on, be nothing but honest with yourself.

There is no change without honesty. Back in 2008, I still remember watching Tony Robbins on that stage in London as he wrote on a flip chart in big, black letters

"The truth will set you free".

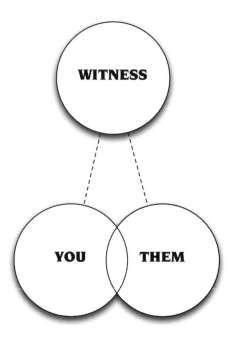

I had never heard the phrase before and I remember vividly, in that moment, realising just how many lies I was telling myself to maintain my illusion of happiness. And then it was like that illusion just dropped away, as if suddenly I could see the trick behind the magic and, no matter how hard I tried, I couldn't un-see it.

It wasn't easy to begin with. I upset myself regularly. I upset other people occasionally (especially those who had enjoyed having a more submissive Brian as a friend) and every so often I tried to pretend the old illusions were still real. But now I knew that I was pretending. The truth was chasing me and it was fast! A transformation was underway and the catalyst was truth.

An important caveat here, honesty is not necessarily about telling your boss exactly what you think of their management technique or finding everyone who ever hurt you in your life and telling them how bad they made you feel. Begin telling the truth to you, about you, and then doing everything that needs to be done to get your life where you want it to be. This will often mean some really hard conversations and some really big decisions about relationships, friendships, careers, directions, locations and your whole future but, let me ask, if you don't make these decisions now, when are you going to make them?

It's time for you to put you first.

I have lost count of the number of people who tell me that they live for their kids or their partner or their work or their mum or anyone/thing apart from themselves. They tell me it *has* to be this way, there can be no other way it can be and to change anything would be selfish. Yes. You are totally right. It would be selfish. And that is *exactly* why it works.

Being selfish does not mean being uncaring. In fact, what if I said that being selfish was perhaps one of the most amazing, kind and inspiring things you can ever do for all the people who love you and care for you?

Right this very second, it's time for you to look after yourself and now I'm going to show you how to do it.

In a nutshell

- You have three viewpoints you can use for any situation or problem – You, Them and Witness.

- Being 'you' is good for making decisions that impact your life but rubbish for being empathic or gauging other people's feelings.

- Being 'them' is good for empathy, seeing things in new ways and working out how to influence others but rubbish for making decisions and looking after yourself.

- Being 'witness' allows you space to solve your own problems and can help make difficult decisions but it is rubbish for actually being caring, nurturing or having any type of connection.

- The ultimate goal is to find a balance of all three.

- When you are stuck, ask yourself which viewpoint you haven't used. You can use the witness viewpoint to find out.

Who's bubble is the right bubble? – revisited

The idea of 'bubble jumping' is one of the big exercises we do on the second day of the Breakthrough Weekend, the course that is the inspiration behind this book. When Erin started ranting about her mum's behavior on the morning of day two, I knew I that this was the perfect scenario to demonstrate the power of bubble jumping to the group.

At first I asked Erin to see the whole incident through her bubble and nothing really changed. She told me how she felt like a child and that she should be allowed to be 20 and have fun and do what she wanted. The anger was still very much there even though we were now several hours away from the events of last night.

Then I asked her to climb inside her mum's bubble. It took her a little bit of work to get her settled into this unfamiliar concept and have her speak to me as her mum would. The first thing we noticed was that in order to really see the world from her mum's perspective, Erin had to allow her anger to drop away.

I asked her 'Why did you keep on calling and looking for Erin last night?' and you should note that it hugely increases the effectiveness of being in someone else's bubble if you ask yourself the questions as if you were that person.

Erin answered 'To find out where she was'.

'And why did you want to find out where she was?'

'I was worried because she hadn't got in touch with me'.

'And why do you want her to get in touch with you when she's out?'

'Because anything could happen and I just want to know she's safe'

'Ok, and why do you want to know she's safe?'

The next few words slipped out of Erin's mouth before she even realised what she'd said, closely followed by a little trickle of tears.

'Because I love her'.

I find that people do many crazy things in the name of love and very few of them that are ever designed to deliberately hurt, embarrass or anger. In that moment, Erin realised it too!

It's easy to get angry or upset when people don't do the things we want them to. Then again, if they always did all the things we wanted them to, they wouldn't be 'them', would they?

Maybe we should just accept that we all have our own ways of doing things and start to notice that, behind every action, there is only ever a positive intention.

My favourite client

I know I probably shouldn't admit it, but in all my years of working with clients, I do have one who will always have a special place in my thoughts.

A good few years before I met her, when she was perhaps about 15, she received a school report from one of her guidance teachers that stated, and I quote, '. . . she will achieve exactly what she deserves from life, i.e. nothing'. As you would expect at 15, her mind did not process this report well and created all sorts of rules due to the Big Bang of this experience.

The reason for this report was a perceived lack of effort but now we know that our perceptions are often flawed. No one had taken the time to discover the difficult circumstances 'behind the scenes' that may explain that lack of effort; her Dad losing his job, the regular bullying at school, the lack of any idea of what she would do when she left school and several others too. All these reasons, that no one had taken the time to notice, shifted her focus elsewhere and eventually led to that report.

Due to all of these early life experiences, of which the report card was one of the most hurtful, one particular rule became an established influence on her life. . . .

"I am stupid."

Because of this rule there seemed no reason to put in the effort for a future that was uncertain. Why be ambitious? Why dream of better? Why think you have any influence over your world at all when all your experiences tell you different? She wasn't one of those people that good things happen to. Her job was to survive and make the best of what she had.

To that end, she was a hard worker and, by the time I met her, life was moving along quite nicely. She had a strong set of friends, her family were supportive and loving and she was a respected, long term member of the crew at her local McDonalds.

And then things changed a little. She fell pregnant at 23 and, as her bump grew, she was given the chance to start doing more office work and in-store training. She thrived in this new environment, displaying a real talent for engaging people and motivating them. Two years later, after the birth of her second child, she accepted an offer to take her new role out to other stores nationwide. She wasn't making huge amounts of money but as she travelled up and down the country on the bus, she was very content to be doing more than she ever thought possible and earning more than she thought she deserved.

She had, she thought, reached her peak.

However, not long after her new job started she was having a conversation with her partner's Dad and she unwittingly let one of her rules spill out on to the table! In a conversation about the future, she uttered a line that would change her life forever. . . .

"People like me don't go to university."

And nothing was ever the same again.

6

Just being you

WHO THE HELL ARE YOU?

Have you ever been in a situation where you realise that you are wearing a mask to hide what is really going on? How many times have you done or said something but then felt regret, anxiety, or guilt because of what everyone else makes of it?

I know that feeling!

I remember as I grew up I was constantly trying to be someone else, wrestling with an internal battle between the Brian I thought I should be and the Brian I actually wanted to be. I always wanted to be cool and fun to be around, I wanted to be respected and loved, but I was so worried about being rejected that it was difficult for me to feel anything except fear.

As I reached my late teenage years, I began to adopt 'personalities', changing my accent or playing a character, that allowed me to show off a version of myself that was funny and sharp and entertaining while, at the same time, perfectly hiding and protecting all of my vulnerability, anxiety and awkwardness.

When I put on the character of Pat the Irish carpet seller (don't ask!) I had permission to be funny and play the clown – this was the fun I craved. However in reality, Pat was protection. If Pat wasn't funny then that was fine, he was just a funny personality with a silly Irish accent. Brian was safe and sound behind his mask.

There always had to be character, because Brian couldn't be funny on his own.

For the same reasons, in my teens and early twenties, I looked to outside sources such as drink and drugs to enable me to be that person I wanted to be. False confidence and bravado were easy to purchase but were only temporary shields from a reality I couldn't escape. You now understand of course that these characters, along with alcohol, etc, were my medications, numbing a set of negative feelings I didn't know how to control.

Perhaps you recognise parallels in your own life?

So, let me ask you this . . . what masks do you wear? Do you put a big smile on in work even though you hate it? Have you become an expert at pretending your relationship is loving and happy when actually you want out and have done for some time? Where do you hide?

To keep myself hidden, my characters had to constantly evolve. As we have discussed, the effects of any medication will wear off with time – as I grew up and found myself in new situations with new people, it became more difficult to protect that 'real' Brian.

For example, when I started working in finance, the business world wouldn't have accepted 'Brian the clown' who found a natural habitat working the pubs and clubs during my early 20s. It was time for a new character and this new character was 'Brian the trainer', the guy who could stand up in front of a room full of people and teach them about tax and stocks, even making it interesting and entertaining. This felt great but was really only another mask. Brian the trainer had a secret. He was completely scripted.

It's easy to be yourself when you have notes on how to do it, isn't it!? I mean, if I could script your day and tell you what to say and when to say it then life would be so much easier, wouldn't it? That was my secret in those days.

I had an average of three months to prepare a script to deliver about three weeks of training. I called it 'scripted spontaneity' – it looked like I was making it up on the spot but, in reality, it had been prepared for weeks. If you ever attended the same course more than once you would hear the same jokes and apparent ad-libs, in the same places, every single time!

I should probably admit at this point that to a certain extent I still do this and when you come to my seminars and courses, you'll often hear a familiar joke or two! A joke that works will be used again and again but there's a big difference . . . back then the joke wasn't just a joke. Back then, the joke was a shield.

And this was my life. Everything I did, even at 30 years old, was about fitting in, being liked and accepted, never rocking the boat, just trudging on, head down, everything might work out but only if I was lucky. I was proudly wearing the 'same sh*t, different day' t-shirt.

Yet I knew there was another me, a different me, the 'real' Brian. He was the same one from when I was a teenager and it was still trapped inside, desperate to escape from all the pretending. I just didn't know how to make that escape or if it was even possible. I was completely stuck in the illusion that I had no control over my thoughts.

I know I am not alone in this experience. I know that in your own life, you have had experiences like this and that's why taking this time to learn how to make your life the best it can possibly be is something of which you should be very proud.

It is critical that right here, as you read the rest of this chapter, you commit to making a change in your life and never going back. Even if your life is already basking under a rainbow of awesomeness, I want you to notice where it is time to make change happen.

With all you have learned in this wee book, you have the knowledge to change your life.

But there is one critical thing that will make the difference between those people who *say* they will change and those who actually *will* change.

RELEASING YOUR VOICE

Do a quick count of all the self help books you have bought. 10? 20? 50? more? Some may have been useful, some less so but I can promise you that, even if this is the first self help book you have ever read, if you commit to it will be the last you'll ever need!

I want you to realise that everything, and I mean *everything*, you need to succeed you already have in you right now. If you take the time and learn how to access even a small portion of what you have inside, you can change anything you want to change.

I don't care who you are and what your situation is because, to be honest, it doesn't actually matter! All that matters is that you realise that you have access to an endless store of confidence, happiness, pride, courage, freedom, security, knowledge and any other feeling you could ever need inside you, right now. That's pretty cool isn't it? What's the catch you say?

Well . . . each of these feelings needs you to take some sort of step towards making it happen. You cannot be passive in your journey to being amazing! When you put the effort in, your mind will be ready to help and drive you to fulfil your purpose on this earth.

All that needs to happen is that you need to start using it.

So, off you go. Good luck. Let me know how you get on.

. . .

. . .

I'm waiting . . .

. . .

. . .

Have you moved yet?

. . .

. . .

Why are you still here?!!

Now, this is where many self help books have a problem. They tell you all this amazing information and then fail completely at helping people actually use it in their own lives. So, with this in mind, allow me to finish of this book by showing you some ways you can begin to think and feel differently and ultimately act differently. The first one is simple. . . .

Practice

THE SECRET OF CHAMPIONS

So many people stay stuck because they try and change huge things in unrealistic timescales and ultimately set themselves up for disappointment.

I used to offer four hour coaching appointments until I realised that people thought they could come along and change their relationship, career, financial situation, past, future, parents, partner, house, kitchen cupboard arrangements, weight, motivation and their destiny for heaven or hell, in four hours!! It's just not possible!

You cannot go from a size 18 to a size 10 in six weeks unless you have freaky genes, an amazing surgeon or make yourself ill, so really you need to stop bloody trying! In the same way you cannot go from a life that has been allowed to slide out of control for years to total, unbridled happiness without taking care of some business along the way.

Many personal development gurus claim that the quick fix is the only way forward but let me be honest with you, people who succeed with quick fixes are the exception, not the rule.

For most of us, change takes time. Or to be more precise, changing your life need only take a second, but changing the *circumstances* of your life takes time.

For example, if you decide that from this point forward it is going to be different and you make happiness your sole purpose, you will change your life right now. That decision has taken less than a second, but integrating the consequences of that decision into the circumstances of your life – your career, relationship and everything else will take a little longer. Here's the thing . . . if you have really decided to change, you *will* do it. If you take that decision honestly and fully commit to it, nothing can stop you.

So let's begin now. Let's dip into your pool of resources and bring something out.

A quick experiment in confidence

Wherever you are sitting just now, sit up a bit straighter, take a couple of nice, deep natural breaths and gently pull your shoulders back to open up your chest. You don't have to make big noticeable movements if you are somewhere public, just do as much as you can wherever you are.

Now, with your eyes open or closed, whatever is more comfortable for you, imagine in your mind's eye a picture of you being as confident as you have ever wanted to be. Really imagine how you would see the world around you differently if you felt totally confident now, at this moment.

Think about what your internal voice would say, and how it would say it, if you had full access to all the confidence you have ever wanted now. Allow yourself to fully immerse yourself in the experience of being where you are right now, feeling quietly and perfectly confident inside. It's not that anyone else would know . . . this confidence is just for you.

I know it might feel a little forced or false, even a bit silly but trust me and stick with it for just a few more seconds. Stay like that, breathing naturally, back straight, shoulders back, keep that image of the confident you in your head, and give it about 10–15 seconds before you read on. . . .

. . .

Don't rush it . . . take all the time you need. . . .

. . .

If you have followed my instructions and allowed yourself to go with it, you will now be feeling confident. No question about it.

If you're not, that's ok, let's figure out what's stopped you imagining, feeling and letting yourself be confident. Perhaps you listened too closely to that wee voice that said 'This is silly, you can't feel confident just like that' or perhaps you have a rule that quite simply says 'I don't know how to be confident'. What was it that stopped you and more importantly . . . why?

Figure it out, go back and do the exercise again and don't let it bloody stop you this time!

This is what is known as 'practice'.

I often have the opportunity to ask kids what confidence is – many of them tell me it is the ability to do things without being scared. When I get this answer I never hesitate to firmly tell them they are completely wrong! Confidence is about being scared and being able to do it anyway. The belief that you can't be scared and confident at the same time is a very common misconception people make and it can very easily cause them to become 'stuck'.

And the best way to become 'not scared' of something is to practise it again and again and again.

So, if you are scared of confidence, you're not going to make that fear go away by simply avoiding it. Similarly, if you are scared of interviews, you aren't going to get better at them by just not applying for jobs. The more practice you get at something that scares you, the better you get at it and the more confident you will be.

Remember, every time you do something another wee pearl of memory joins your string and your mind begins to learn. The more you practise, the more you learn. The more you learn, the easier it becomes.

So my first tip to making this book be your catalyst for change is to practise one thing every day, especially when it feels difficult or you feel like giving up. Practise making decisions until you are good at making decisions then switch and practise being confident until you are good at being confident and so on. Become good at something and then something else and then before you know it, you'll be good at loads of things!

Practise changing your thoughts rather than medicating your feelings, avoiding your triggers and pushing yourself to do things your mind is not ready to do. Learn your code, listen for your rules, be aware of you internal pictures and practise just being YOU.

Without doubt, if you want to make progress, plenty of practise is a great way to go about it. But there are times in life when a much more direct approach is required. I call that . . .

THE NIKE APPROACH

Remember our equation

$$\textbf{Thought = Feeling = Action}$$

Well, we've talked about thoughts; we've talked about feelings, now we need to talk about taking action.

One of my biggest frustrations within the world of personal development is the so called 'Law of Attraction'. While it has certainly introduced people to the power of dreaming, vision boarding, wishing for a brighter future and has given millions of people hope, bizarrely these are also the very reasons why the whole concept upsets me!

Dreaming and boarding and wishing and hoping don't make things happen. Yes, they make you feel good and, if they trigger your code, they can definitely help you get motivated, but your vision board alone can't get you the job, the body, the car, the relationship, the future that you want.

The only way that can happen is if YOU make it happen.

You may very well believe with all your heart that the universe is listening to your desires and dreams but consider this . . . if you are right, don't you also think the universe is watching to see if you are serious and willing to take action?

Reading a self-help book is safe. Nothing has to change if you are just reading a book. Doing a vision board is safe. Waiting for the universe to deliver your desires is safe. It means it's not your fault if you don't get what you want. It can just be the will of the universe. This is the ultimate absolution of personal responsibility.

As you read these words I want to teach you how to change your life. And it starts, right here, right now. And it starts small.

**Miracles are measured in miles
but they are achieved in inches.**

THE LONGEST JOURNEY

I tell the story about my old masks often because I find the theme resonates with many people; my life was not where I wanted it to be and I had no idea how to change it. So I just hid from it.

I'm sure it's obvious to you that, if I am now writing this book . . . something must have changed!

In 2003, 'Brian the trainer', was exposed to the world of personal development when I was sent on a training course by my boss. I had no idea what to expect and the whole experience was going to be totally new to me. To be honest, I didn't even know what the course was actually about!

I had never given personal development a second thought. I thought it sounded weird, difficult, time consuming and a bit silly. It definitely wasn't for me. Of course, I had no experience at all on which to base any of these assumptions – they were all totally made up to keep me safe. Up to that point I thought that life was always going to be full of masks and my past would be a constant weight around my neck. I would be a survivor of life, a passenger that looked on while everyone else succeeded. I was doing the bare minimum I needed to do in order to survive and modestly succeed.

On that course, I was given an amazingly simple insight that I have never forgotten. . . .

It didn't have to be that way.

I discovered I had the power to change my thoughts, manage my feelings and do things I never dreamed possible and it was intoxicating!

Now, I'm not saying I came away from that first training course and life was all roses and butterflies. Actually, it was after that course that the hard work really started.

Within six weeks of that course I was married, my new wife experienced a huge panic attack on our honeymoon and had to go home, leaving me with our two kids in Paris. Then the day I returned home we were told that my dad was terminally ill. It was an interesting few weeks to say the least! I didn't realise it at the time but all the new skills I had learned were being given the sternest possible test.

Of course I was neither skilled nor experienced at this point so I muddled my way through one of the most turbulent, emotional times of my life by just doing *stuff*! I had no idea if I was doing the *stuff* right, I just knew I had to keep doing something. To be honest with you, I was making it up as I went along. There are some who might argue that I still am! I knew one thing though – I couldn't stop for fear my whole life would fall apart.

I completely refused to give in and just stop, giving up was never an option, and this is the test that will prove if you are ready to change your life forever: Can you remember what you have learned and practise it even when the world turns round and hits you harder than you've ever been hit before?

Your destiny will not be defined by how many times life hits you, all of us have experienced life turning round and giving us a smack between the eyes. Your destiny will be defined by what you do about it when it happens.

Everyone has challenges but you can't wear your pain like a badge of honour and expect to be rewarded for it. You will be rewarded for courage, resilience and living a life of purpose. That is where destiny is made.

I am asking you right now to realise that this whole book has been about one understanding:

YOU are in charge.

I have used the metaphor of weight loss a few times through this book and, if this is something that has affected your life, I bet you will have sometimes pretended that you have no control over it. You'll say you had no choice, or that the chocolate biscuits were speaking to you, or that someone made you eat them, or that because the pack was in the house you had to eat the whole lot just to get rid of them. But we all know that's rubbish! All of these are choices. *Your* choices.

So let me ask you a key question:

Who do you see when you look at yourself in the mirror?

Just think about that for a moment . . . really *think* about it.

Do you look in the mirror and like the person staring back at you? Or do you pick yourself apart, criticising every blemish, bump or imperfection? Do you look into your eyes and see failure, sadness, guilt or fear? If you do this, is it any wonder you don't care if you eat that whole packet of chocolate biscuits, get the success you want or have the relationship you want?

What if *you* are the source of the pain that you need to comfort with your medication. What if it's your own negative perception of yourself that keeps you stuck?

And what if there's another way?

How would it feel if you could look in the mirror in the morning and see the real you? And don't try to tell me that the pain and the suffering you see is the real you. It's not.

The real you is the 'you' that wants to be loved and cared for, that wants happiness and success, that wants to be respected and make decisions.

Even if you feel you are the only one that sees how amazing you are just now, that's OK. Remember, miracles are measured in miles but are achieved in inches.

What if you could look in the mirror and see the kindness, love, gratitude, care, happiness, safety, and all the other things that are important to you? What if you looked in the mirror and started loving the person looking back at you?

I mean, imagine if you woke up tomorrow and decided that you were going to love yourself (or, at the very least, think you were alright!). Would it not be easier to lose weight, stop smoking, go for the promotion or have the relationship you want?

If you stopped criticising yourself for every little thing you did wrong and started being kind to yourself, would it not be so much easier to take care of yourself, to realise that you are important, to accept that you matter, and start doing what you need to do to be the absolute best you?

I know that you may not be where you want to be right now. That's OK. Every journey starts somewhere. One more time, miracles are measured in miles but are achieved in inches.

And some inches are much more difficult to achieve than others.

MOVING THAT INCH

Let's jump forward to 2007, four years after our wedding, and a short but life changing conversation is about to happen. I was in EuroDisney with my family, and we were celebrating because, after all the drama of our honeymoon and what had happened in the weeks and months after it, this was a trip of recovery.

My wife was now happy and those panic attacks were a thing of the past (thanks to living by her code and letting go of a couple of significant Big Bang memories). We were having the honeymoon we were meant to have had four years earlier. This trip was equally, if not even more important.

It was on a bed in a wee Disney branded chalet, surrounded by my family, that I finally made the decision to follow my heart, leave the secure confines of my job with one of the biggest financial institutions in the UK and start my own business. HeadStrong was born!

The first inch had been moved and, let me tell you, it was one of the easiest decisions I've ever made. I knew exactly why I was leaving and that meant I was actually far more excited than scared.

And now the tough inches started.

Let me be clear. When I started HeadStrong I had nothing. No clients, no money, no clue. Just a passionate desire to help.

It is that passion that gave me purpose and made all the subsequent, tough inches possible. Every time I hit a challenge, I had an unwavering belief that what I was doing was right. I remember things got so tight at one point, I was working out just how much I would earn if I returned to work at my local supermarket on minimum wage. I wondered if I could keep the business going and work part time just to make some cash. But that move never felt right. It seemed that would have been a step backwards. And backwards is never a direction you want to go when you are looking to achieve your dream.

I never lost sight of where I was going and most importantly, all the way through this, I had a belief that I could and would make it. This doesn't mean I arrogantly wandered into meetings believing I was the 'man'!! Far from it! I had absolutely no clue how I was going to achieve what I wanted to achieve. I just knew that I wanted to get there and had one rule that kept me going through all of this. I would not stop until I had made it.

A fundamental rule of success – always be moving forward.

Think about all the times you've wanted to change something in your life and I bet, as you look back at them now, you spot the pattern we talked about before – when you were doing what *you* wanted to do, you were happy. The unhappiness and discomfort started the second you stopped moving forward and became stuck again. When you do what *you* want to do there can only be one outcome and that outcome is happiness.

But in order to do what *you* want to do you will have to re-prioritise where you are in your life.

So many of us put ourselves second, maybe even third best in our lives and every single day we feel it. Every single day we know we are not being true. Every single day we know we are hiding. Every single day we know we are making ourselves less than we are.

Imagine now, just imagine, how it would be if that wasn't true anymore. And don't you tell me you can't! There is a difference between 'I can't' and 'I won't'!

Not putting yourself first affects every area of your life – relationships, career, money, everything and I want you, as you reach the end of this book, to make a decision to change that.

Again, it's all about the inches.

I want you to start asking yourself three simple questions that will give you clarity on your decisions and begin a process of being wonderfully selfish! The following simple, life changing questions ensure that you put 'you' first.

Any time you have a decision to make, ask them in this order and, if you answer 'No' to any of the three, then you need to question what it is you are doing and why it is you are doing it.

1. Is this something that is OK for me to do?

2. If I do this thing, is it OK for the people I care about?

3. If I do this thing, is it OK for anyone I will come into contact with while I do it?

In 2008, just after leaving that secure job, I got the big break-through that is the driver behind this book and so many things I do. I finally learned to like being me.

I flew to London to see some guy called Tony Robbins. I had heard a lot about him and I had tried to listen to his CDs but never really got into them. I had never seen him live and was preparing myself for a highly polished, Americanised, perfectly stage managed performance. I thought it would be a carefully choreographed and scripted stage show.

I was wrong.

On the first morning of the course, I remember walking in and thinking I'd entered a nightmare! Every single one of my rules were being broken by every single person in the room and I could feel the fear hit me instantly! People were dancing, hugging, cheering.

Everyone was going crazy! I felt instantly and unbearably uncomfortable. This was not what I expected, this was chaos!

A thought flew through my head, it was one of my rules, "I'm going to look silly". I didn't have a character to protect me in this situation. I had the wrong mask on and I didn't have time to change it. The people I was with knew me as the NLP trainer and coach. That was the mask I was wearing and I had to live up to that expectation. But, in this extreme and unexpected situation, I had no idea how I should act. I didn't want to look stupid in their eyes but at the same time I wanted to immerse myself in the experience.

Due to this internal battle, the first few hours were hard and the bizarre requests kept on coming from the stage;

"I want you to Dance like Britney Spears" (it was 2008, remember!).
"Turn and give the person to your left a massage."
"Get three awesome hugs before you take a seat."

Each of these experiences compounded my fears as I danced, massaged and hugged while, inside, feeling anxious and conflicted at every turn. But I was also enthralled and slowly I began to change.

I watched for three days and took part in every crazy, ridiculous thing he asked me to do. By the end of the course, I was desperate to dance, hungry for hugs and loving the massages. I felt free. A master was at work and I didn't just want to watch him, I wanted to BE him!!

I knew his tools and I knew I had them. And it wasn't all show. Yes, it was choreographed but it didn't seem overly scripted. In everything I watched, Tony came across as honest, passionate and charming. He had a way of explaining things that was simple, disarming, funny and powerful.

He made mistakes. I didn't think mistakes were allowed.

And he swore, a lot! Is that ok? Can you do that? Is that in the rules?

As I soaked it all in, I realised I had been too busy trying to get everything absolutely perfect. But here I wasn't watching perfect, I was watching passion. A new picture was forming inside my mind. Unknown to me, a new rule was being created deep inside my mind.

On the final day of the course, a piece of music came on the huge speakers at the front of the room next to where we were now standing. It was a piece of music called the Mingulay Boat Song, a song my dad used to sing, and to me, in that moment, it felt like a message. I stood there in that room, eyes tightly closed, running pictures of an amazing future, loudly singing words to a song that no-one else knew, tears streaming down my face and it was there, right in that very moment, that I realised how awesome life could be without masks.

I didn't care who heard me sing, I didn't care who saw me cry, I didn't care about anything else apart from me, my family and my purpose.

And here we are now, many years since that day singing the Mingulay Boat Song and it has never changed. There are *no* rules that define what I can or cannot do, there are no more 'shoulds' and there are no reasons why life can't be just the way I want it.

And this is my message to you.

I have given you my story in this chapter not because I want to impress you but to impress *upon* you[1] that everyone has stuff, everyone has baggage, everyone has struggles and everyone has the ability to get over them and live a life of meaning and purpose.

I am not special, or unique or different from you. I just did what I had to do. I changed the blueprint of my mind to make it work for me rather than against me.

Now is your time. Your story is already being written and it's time to make it an adventure rather than a tragedy!! It is time to stop waiting for permission and to start living the life you want rather than the life you are settling for.

This last exercise brings everything you have learned in this book into one place. Even if it hurts, please answer honestly and candidly. It is time to decide *your* future, not the future others tell you should have. Even if you haven't done it up to now, write this one down. It's important. You owe it to yourself to give this ten minutes out of your day.

---

[1] Thanks Tony!

Designing the future

1. If you could do anything with your life from this moment forward what would you do? List at least five things.

2. What has stopped you doing each of these in the past?

3. What can you do now to start making these things a reality? (Remember: miracles are measured in miles, but achieved in inches. It is absolutely OK to start slowly.)

4. How does the thought of achieving these things make you feel?

5. If there is any fear, what is its intention? What specifically is it that you are scared of?

6. If you could get advice from someone else, alive or dead, who would it be? And what would that advice be? What stops you taking that advice?

7. Would it be OK to start living your own life, and your own dreams, now?

8. Do you deserve happiness?

9. What would you have to fully accept as true to feel as if you could achieve all your dreams?

10. If you were to start with one of your dreams, which one would it be? And what is the first inch you would need to conquer?

YOUR TURN NOW

There are NO rules about who you should be or what you need to do with your life. You can have the life you want and all it takes is for you to move that first tiny inch in the right direction. You have that power.

Throughout this book you have learned that your reality happens inside your mind. You have learned that feelings do not happen on their own; they are driven by thoughts that have taken a lifetime to create.

You have learned that, if the universal formula of cause and effect is right, the actions you take in life are merely an effect. The cause is your thoughts and that means your destiny is ultimately defined by your thoughts. If you change how you think, you *will* change how you feel and if you change how you feel you *will* change how you act. The way you act will guide your life and your destiny.

You don't need a Tony Robbins for you to find permission to be you. You know what? You don't even need a Brian Costello for that.

You just need you.

Put yourself first, make decisions and don't sacrifice your desires for everyone else.

Start liking, even loving yourself.

This doesn't mean hours in front of a mirror admiring yourself or telling everyone how fabulous you are! You can quietly and genuinely appreciate yourself. Be proud of who you are. When you think about your story, it's pretty amazing that you are here, doing what you are doing, living the life you have. Some of your inches have been difficult but you have kept going. You have survived everything the world has thrown at you and here you are, reading a book that you hope will make sense of it all and make it better.

You know what that means?

That means you are already doing the one thing you need to do to change your life.

You have taken action.

And now it is time to take more.

You have everything you need to move your next inch as soon as you close this book.

I wonder what awesome thing you'll decide to do next?

I hope you always remember to simply . . .

Do good things.

Chapter 6 in a nutshell:

- All you need to achieve all you want is inside you right now.

- Your life is your responsibility and, now you have read this book, you now know how easy it is to start taking control.

- Take it slow. Miracles are measured in miles and achieved in inches. Tiny steps now will train your mind for success and enable you to take huge strides later.

- You matter, you are important, you deserve happiness.

- Action creates change. Go do something awesome.

- You are loved.

My favourite client – revisited

I don't know if it just a Scottish thing but many people I meet prefer to prepare for failure rather than dream of success. The reason they give me for this apparent self-sabotage is that it is easier to deal with failure if you are prepared for it in advance. My opinion is that failure becomes much more likely if that is all you think about. Let me ask if you would feel comfortable if the pilot of your plane came over the speakers before your flight and told you how he or she was going to do their best to get you to your destination but they couldn't promise anything?

Success is born of hope. If your perception of life tells you that there is no hope then success will just feel like luck. Personally, I like to create my own luck.

In the hour following her rules spilling out all over the lunch table, my favourite client had her world shook up. Her belief that people like her didn't go to university was so perfectly challenged that a thought popped into her head that, just maybe, there may be a version of her future she had never considered before. That thought was allowed to grow so strong that, not long after that original conversation, she was enrolled in a degree at university.

It wasn't an easy ride! Everything she was doing was rattling on her belief that she was stupid. Within the first weeks of her new course she nearly dropped out because 'it was silly to think I could do something like this'. But she didn't. She kept going. There was a new, powerful rule forming. She was starting to believe perhaps people like her could do anything they wanted.

In the end this 'stupid' girl walked away from university with a first class honours degree in microbiology and was recognised as 'most distinguished student' in the entire school of science not once, but twice. She was enthusiastically offered the chance to study for her PhD but she declined. A new dream had emerged.

Dreams are powerful things because, once you start having them, it's really difficult to stop! It's amazing how much energy and drive you create when the thoughts inside your head fit your code.

After all her experiences in school, the new dream was to be a teacher and make sure that no young person ever had the experience she had. And, if you go find her today, that's exactly what she is doing. That teacher was almost right when she was 15, she did get everything she deserved. She now has everything she deserved for all her hard work, all her effort, all her talent, all her dreams.

She is by far my favourite client because of just how far she has come, how much she has grown, and how she continues to dream. She is also my wife, so I accept I may be a little biased!

This is, as you might expect, a very personal story for me to tell but I recount this story to have the opportunity to tell you that Sheena is also not magic or special. She is just like you and me. Her secret was to have a dream and never give up. You can do that too.

I remember hearing the actor Ashton Kutcher (I know! I wasn't expecting it to be him either!) talk about his career when he said that 'Opportunity looks a lot like hard work'. I hope that you can take inspiration from Sheena's story, and all the stories you have read here, and realise that change requires honesty, hard work and the desire to do whatever it takes.

Remember, miracles are measured in miles but they are achieved in inches. Not all of those inches will be easy but each one of them is a step towards your own, personal miracle.

Make it happen.

I promised I'd remember, did you?

Just before you go, I wonder how many times you came across the Number 23?

And did you spot the red shoes?

The mind is simply amazing at finding random things – all you have to do is ask.

Now you've found the red shoes, what are you going to ask your mind to find next?

–B